THE 12 STEP WORKBOOK

A compilation of many authors and contributors.

Edited and compiled by Charlotte and Bob B.

Published by:
CJB Publishing
16458 Bolsa Chica St. #147
Huntington Beach CA 92649
FrazierChar@yahoo.com

Copyright 2021
First Printing, 2022

Printed in the United States of America

ISBN: 9798795480213

All references to *Alcoholics Anonymous Pages* in this workbook are from the *Fourth Edition publication, by Alcoholics Anonymous World Services, Inc.*

Book Shepherding/Editing/Formatting – Mike Rounds www.PublishersHaven.com

Cover Design – Leslie Sears www.lesismore.us

Table of Contents

DEDICATION

This Workbook is lovingly dedicated to my husband, Bob B. And who had an unwavering belief in this process changing his life. When we found these people that it is exactly what it did for him and many others.

Thank you for what you did with your dash. Born November1945 passed away October 2004, six days before his 18th sober anniversary.

As I sit here today so many years later, I have the feeling that God put Bob in my life at the dance in Long Beach so that later in our sobriety we would be given the gift of dedication to helping people work the 12 Steps as outlined in the Big Book of Alcoholics Anonymous. After we collected information from our friends in Colorado, Joe H. and Don P., and attended a Joe McQ. and Charlie P. workshop, Bob wanted to facilitate a workshop in our apartment. Afterwards, Bob said if we were going to continue doing this, we needed to put both the worksheets and Joe and Charlie's language together in a book. It took us over four months to complete it! And that notebook is now this 12 Step Workbook.

With all my love, Charlotte

ABOUT THE AUTHORS

I met Bob in AA in 1987. Although we were sober and being sponsored, we still suffered from old relationship behaviors. We wanted to change our lives and live the 12 Steps, but we weren't sure how we were actually going to take the Steps, how we were going to work the Steps in our lives. In 1988 we went to a Round Up in Torrance, California and met Joe H who was sponsored by Don P in Colorado. We asked Joe to give us a copy of the worksheets and he said come back tomorrow and I will bring you one. That happened and he gave us the flyer for the Joe and Charlie Big Book Comes Alive Workshop in 1988 in Santa Monica. We went with people from our 705 Club group, and they were as impressed as we were and they wanted us to hold a workshop. The first workshop happened in the spring of 1989 in our home and the 12 Steps changed our lives and our relationship.

ABOUT THE 12 STEP WORKBOOK

The reason I am publishing the 12 Step Workbook is this: The 12 Steps and this Workbook changed my life, Bob's life, and our marriage, and they can change your life and relationships, too. With willingness and determination, you can become happy, joyous, and free.

The 12 Steps, first published in *Alcoholics Anonymous* in 1939[1], are a "group of principles, spiritual in their nature, which, if practiced as a way of life, can expel the obsession to drink and enable the sufferer to become happily and usefully whole."[2]

We may read about the 12 Steps in the Big Book (AA members' nickname for the book *Alcoholics Anonymous*) and we may hear about the 12 Steps in meetings, but how exactly do we take and then integrate the 12 Steps into our lives? This Workbook is a companion to the Big Book and will help you understand and work all the steps! It has already helped approximately 50,000 people suffering from alcoholism and many other addictions since my husband and I began using it as the basis for a 17-week workshop in 1989.

It can be used by a recovering person alone and shared with a counselor or spiritual advisor, by a sponsor and a sponsee working as a team, or by many people coming together in a workshop setting. It works, it really does!

---

[1] Quotations in this 12 Step Workbook attributed to the Big Book are from *Alcoholics Anonymous*, Fourth Edition, © 2001, Alcoholics Anonymous World Services, Inc.

[2] From the Forward to *Twelve Steps and Twelve Traditions*, © 1952, 1953, 1981 by The A.A. Grapevine, Inc. and Alcoholics Anonymous Publishing (now known as Alcoholics Anonymous World Services, Inc.).

DISCLAIMER

Throughout this workbook, references are made to pages in "The Big Book" *4th Edition publication, by Alcoholics Anonymous World Services, Inc.*

The reference pages cited assume that the reader is using either a printed version (recommended) or, if an electronic, downloaded version, that it is in PDF format.

If the version being used is in the *Kindle*® format, the page number references will NOT be valid due to Amazon's "flowable text" used in the *Kindle*® publishing format.

The printed version of the "The Big Book" may be ordered from Amazon.com at the following URL:

https://www.amazon.com/Alcoholics-Inc-AA-World-Services/dp/B005F1Q9NQ

Instructions for Facilitating a 12 Step program

For those of you who are interested in taking the 12 Steps, but have never done so before, we have included step-by-step instructions for each Step. We have included the pages to read in the Big Book while you are reading The 12 Step Workbook.

Instructions for Individual Sponsors and Sponsees

• Individual Users

• This Workbook can be used by a recovering person alone, but when you get to the working Steps 4 through 12 you will want to consult with a counselor or spiritual advisor to help you complete the work.

• Sponsors and Sponsees

• If you are a sponsor and want to work one-on-one with your sponsee you can also use The 12 Step Workbook.

Instructions for Groups Starting a Workshop

• If you are inclined to facilitate a workshop, my suggestion is to have two recovering people that have been in a workshop prior and have completed the 12 Steps with their sponsor.

• Also the workshops can be facilitated by a man and woman co-ed or two men only or two women only, whatever your group needs.

WEEK 1 – START YOUR STEP WORK

Instructions - Start Your Step Work

• Workbook Read
• BIG BOOK Read - Page xi, Paragraphs 1 and 2
• Workbook Read
• BIG BOOK Read - Page xi, Paragraph 3 to End of Preface
• BIG BOOK Read - Page xiii, Paragraph 1
• Workbook Read
• BIG BOOK Read - Page xiii, Paragraph 2 to End of Forward to First Edition
• BIG BOOK Read - Page xv, Paragraph 1 to Page xvi, Top of Page
• Workbook Read
• BIG BOOK Read - Page xvi, Paragraph 1 to End of Forward to Second Edition
• BIG BOOK Read Forward to Third Edition, Page xxii
• BIG BOOK Read Forward to Fourth Edition, Page xxiii to Page xxiv

ASSIGNMENT: Read "The Doctor's Opinion" (Big Book - Page xxv to Page xxxii) and answer homework questions.

Big Book Workshop Format

Using the Fourth Edition of *Alcoholics Anonymous*

Hello, my name is _____ and I'm an alcoholic. Welcome to the Big Book Workshop. We don't consider ourselves to be the gurus of the Big Book of Alcoholics Anonymous. We don't consider ourselves to be the experts in anything at all. Please join me in a moment of silence to remind us of why we are here, and for the alcoholic who still suffers.

Would you please join me in the Workshop Prayer: **"God, let me set aside everything I think I know about You, AA, Myself, and My Disease for an open mind and a new experience. Let me be honest and thorough. AMEN."**

For the first couple of weeks, we will go around the room and introduce ourselves, to get to know one another.

PRIMARY PURPOSE:

It is the purpose of this Workshop to experience the recovery process as outlined in the Big Book of Alcoholics Anonymous, either for the first time or again, so we may better carry out and understand our primary purpose: to stay sober and carry the message to the still suffering alcoholic. We are here to talk about RECOVERY ONLY, and to go through the Twelve-Step process as outlined in the Big Book of Alcoholics Anonymous. This is not an emotional or intellectual exercise, this is a spiritual exercise, so we can all recover and experience the recovery process as we read the Big Book and The 12 Step Workbook together.

STEP STUDY OUTLINE AND ASSIGNMENT SHEETS

The following is a suggested assignment sheet and outline for use by the Step Study Workshop. The Workshop is a 17-week commitment. It is suggested that before the Step Study is completed, each member will have read the entire text of the Big Book, and will have taken Steps One through Twelve as outlined in the Big Book and the Workbook.

PRELIMINARY MEETING:

The first meeting will follow the outline regarding the purpose, plan, and meeting format of the Step Study. It is important that the commitment section of this outline is carefully reviewed, and that each participant thoroughly understand that he or she is COMMITTING TO TAKING THE STEPS. It is most helpful that everyone is present as much as possible and that communication develops between the team members so that they know how the other team members are progressing and how they are feeling about the Study.

PURPOSE AND PLAN OF WORKSHOP

PURPOSE OF WORKSHOP:

1.   To provide the person who has not worked the Steps with motivation and assistance in "TAKING THE STEPS."

2.   To provide those who have worked the Steps with an opportunity and motivation to do it again and to share their experiences.

PLAN FOR WORKSHOP:

(A)   There will be two leaders who will read the Big Book and The 12 Step Workbook, and who have worked the Steps in the manner described in the Big Book and The 12 Step Workbook. The balance of participants will be members who have never worked the Steps in this manner but who are WILLING to try.

(B)   This Workshop is not like a regular Big Book study meeting. In this Workshop, you will be given assignments to work the 12 Steps and you are asked to share your work with your sponsor.

(C)   At the preliminary meeting all those present will be asked to:

     (1)   COMMIT to stay with the team until we have completed the 12 Steps.

(2)   COMMIT to doing all the Steps according to the Big Book.

(3)   Once you have completed the Workshop, we ask that you COMMIT to do it once again and bring a newcomer with you as part of your Twelfth Step work.

(4)   COMMIT to attend the meetings except in the instance of RARE or EXTREMELY UNUSUAL CIRCUMSTANCES. Each member really needs to be present each week.

(5)   COMMIT to exchange telephone numbers (WOMEN WITH WOMEN AND MEN WITH MEN) and make telephone or personal contact with one or more members of the team during each week the Steps are being taken, and to share your problems or experience with the assignment that week.

MEETING FORMAT:

(A)   The two leaders simply discuss the assigned material and share their experience in applying it to their lives.

(B)   Each member must come to the meeting having read and studied those portions of the Big Book and the "Twelve Steps and Twelve Traditions" which relate to the Step under consideration and having done his or her assignment.

(C)   The purpose of the Workshop will be to apply the principles of each Step in each member's lives.

WE WILL BE READING AT THE PRELIMINARY MEETING:

The Preface, Forewords to the First Edition, Second Edition, Third Edition, and Fourth Edition.

NOTE: The Preface states: This book has become the BASIC TEXT for our Society. The foreword to the First Edition states: To show other alcoholics PRECISELY HOW WE HAVE RECOVERED is the main purpose of this book. Compare this language with the language on Page 29 where it is stated: Further on, CLEAR-CUT DIRECTIONS are given showing how we recovered. This is the task we as a team are about to undertake!

Refer To the Next Page "Big Book Goals"

BIG BOOK GOALS

GOAL 1 Problem	GOAL 2 Solution	GOAL 3 Action Necessary For Recovery
Doctor's Opinion Chap. 1. Bill's Story	Chap. 2. There Is a Solution Chap. 3. More About Alcoholism Chap. 4. We Agnostics	Chap. 5. How It Works Chap. 6. Into Action Chap. 7. Working with Others
STEP ONE	STEP TWO	STEPS THREE through TWELVE

PREFACE

BIG BOOK READ - Page xi, Paragraphs 1 and 2[3]

BASIC TEXT: A textbook is a book that is used to transfer information from the mind of one human being, through the written word, to the mind of another human being, thereby increasing the knowledge of the user of the textbook. A textbook is always written in a certain sequence. It assumes that the reader of the subject matter will know very little about it. It will start at a simple level and as the reader's knowledge increases, the material presented becomes a little more difficult.

The Big Book is a textbook written in standard textbook form. It assumes that we know nothing about the disease of alcoholism. It starts by describing what the problem is. Then it describes the solution. Finally, it gives us a program of action so we can find that solution.

We believe that the Doctor's Opinion and the first four chapters prepare us for Chapter 5. If we go through it this way, we will be able to see how each chapter dovetails into itself, building information on information.

The other idea is that alcoholics haven't changed since 1939. Alcohol hasn't changed. Therefore, we have not found it necessary to change the program of recovery.[4]

BIG BOOK READ - Page xi, Paragraph 3 to End of Preface

FORWARD TO FIRST EDITION

BIG BOOK READ - Page xiii, Paragraph 1

This forward suggests two pertinent ideas:

1.   The Big Book was written by Bill W. and edited by 40 sober people. And more than 100 men and women who have <u>recovered</u> with the information, as set forth in the Big Book. They <u>recovered</u> with the same problems that we have as alcoholics today.

2.   <u>To show other alcoholics precisely how we have recovered is the main purpose of the Big Book</u>. Our Big Book does not deal with membership or fellowship. It deals with <u>recovery only</u>. If we choose to do what the first 100 people did to recover, then we should expect the same results, which is recovery from the disease of alcoholism.

BIG BOOK READ - Page xiii, Paragraph 2 to End of Forward to First Edition

---

[3] Page references throughout the Workbook are to the Fourth Edition of the Big Book.
[4] All commentaries in this Workbook are from the Joe and Charlie 1988 Conference, Santa Monica, CA.

FORWARD TO SECOND EDITION
(Early History of the AA Program)

BIG BOOK READ - Page xv, Paragraph 1 to Page xvi, Top of Page

Dr. Silkworth's Diagnosis of Bill W. from Towns Hospital, New York

From this Doctor, the broker had learned the grave nature of alcoholism. In 1933, Dr. Silkworth treated Bill and explained what he believed to be the disease of alcoholism. He believed:

1. It was not Willpower.
2. It was not a lack of Moral Character.
3. It was not Sin.

He said, "Bill, I believe alcoholism is an actual disease and a peculiar disease.

1. It is a disease of the Body.
2. As well as a disease of the Mind."

The Doctor said, "Bill, when people like you drink, they react entirely differently than normal people. Normal people take a drink and they get a slightly warm comfortable relaxing feeling. They may have one or two drinks and that's all they want to drink. But Bill, people like you drink a drink and you get a physical feeling in your body that produces a physical craving that demands more of the same. When you start, instead of one or two, you end up with three, four, six, until you get drunk, sick, and in trouble. This is abnormal and it only happens to one out of ten people. Therefore, Bill, I'll say that physically you have become allergic to alcohol and react abnormally to it."

"Also, you have developed an Obsession of the Mind. Normal people do not care if they drink or not. They can drink today, tomorrow, a month from now and it's not a big deal to them. People like you, Bill, have developed an obsession of the mind to drink. That obsession is so strong that it will make you believe something that isn't true."

"From time to time you've been told that you can't drink, and from time to time you've known that you can't drink. From time to time, you've even sworn off drinking. But the Obsession of the Mind is an idea that says you can now drink. This time it will be different. This time you'll only take one drink. This obsession is so strong that it makes you believe you can drink and just before you drink you know it's going to be okay. It will always lead you back to taking a drink, then the drink will trigger the Allergy, then you will be unable to stop drinking. People like you have become hopeless."

After this conversation, Bill left the hospital and stayed sober for a while, but his Obsession of the Mind told him that he could drink, and he did. One year later he was put back into that hospital under Dr. Silkworth's care and this time Dr. Silkworth pronounced him incurable. Bill left in the summer of 1934 knowing he could not drink. Fear kept him sober for a while. On Armistice Day

1934, his mind told him he could drink, he took a drink and triggered the allergy and couldn't stop drinking.

Ebby's Contribution

Ebby, who had been in the Oxford Group, came to visit Bill and gave Bill two other pieces of information. Dr. Silkworth had explained the <u>problem</u>. Ebby said, "Bill the <u>solution</u> to that problem is finding a <u>Power Greater than human power</u>. People like us have become absolutely <u>powerless over alcohol</u>. If we are to recover, we must find a <u>Power greater than alcohol</u>, greater than we are, and greater than human power. If human power would have worked, we would have recovered a long time ago. Willpower would have done it, doctors would have done it, ministers would have done it. But none of them have helped us. If we can find a <u>Power greater than human power,</u> then we can recover!"

"The Oxford Group has given me a <u>Practical Program of Action</u> and they guarantee that if I apply it in my life, I will find that Power, and I won't have to drink anymore. Look at me—I've been sober for two months." Bill knew Ebby and how he drank, he knew a miracle had happened in Ebby's life.

From these three pieces of information, Bill <u>recovered</u> from his disease!

1. He learned the <u>Problem</u> from Dr. Silkworth.
2. He learned the <u>Solution</u> from Ebby and the Oxford Group.
3. He received the <u>Practical Program of Action</u>.

He applied the action in his life and found that Power and never had to drink again! He got sober on December 12, 1934 and passed away sober on January 24, 1971. 35 years of sobriety.

BIG BOOK READ - Page xvi, Paragraph 1 to End of Forward to Second Edition

FORWARD TO THIRD EDITION

BIG BOOK READ - Page xxii

FORWARD TO FOURTH EDITION

BIG BOOK READ – Page xxiii to End of Forward to Fourth Edition

- Read "The Doctor's Opinion."
- Answer the questions on "The Doctor's Opinion."
- Begin to write "How you are powerless over alcohol."
- <u>Suggestion</u>: Write a history of your drinking *(i.e.,* starting and stopping on your own and what happened). When you picked up the first thing to change how you felt mentally, physically, from the outside of you. Then, if you stopped and didn't stay stopped, what happened? (*i.e.* wasn't working the Steps or going to meetings. Result: jail, institution, death)?

It is equally important to write any reservations you may have that you are, in fact, powerless over alcohol.

ASSIGNMENT: Answer homework questions for "The Doctor's Opinion"

THE DOCTOR'S OPINON QUESTIONS

BIG BOOK PAGE XXV, PARAGRAPH 1

1. Are you interested in the Doctor's estimate of the physical part of your disease, to discover the fact that you are powerless over alcohol after the first drink?

2. Was the testimony that came from medical men who have had experience with our suffering and our recovery helpful to you?

PARAGRAPH 3

3. Are you the type who is hopeless (wants to quit and can't)?

PARAGRAPH 5

4. Are you the type that other methods failed completely (everything you tried)?

BIG BOOK PAGE XXVI, TOP OF PAGE

5. Are you willing to believe this Book has a remedy for you and can you rely on what these people, who wrote the Book, say about themselves?

PARAGRAPH 2

6. Do you believe that your body is as abnormal as your mind after the first drink?

7. Did any explanation you got from yourself or others, as to why you couldn't control your drinking, satisfy you?

8. Did any picture of you, which left out the **<u>physical factor</u>**, feel incomplete?

PARAGRAPH 3

9. Does the Doctor's theory that you have an allergy to alcohol interest you? Does it make good sense? Does it explain many things that you could not otherwise account for?

BIG BOOK PAGE XXVII, PARAGRAPH 4

10. Do you believe that some form of a spiritual experience is of urgent importance to you? Do you believe that any human can apply the power of good that is needed to produce this spiritual experience?

PARAGRAPH 6

11.   Do you believe more in the Power which has pulled you back from the gates of death than yourself?

BIG BOOK PAGE XXVIII, PARAGRAPH 1

12.   Do you believe that when you put alcohol in your body, the reaction is like an allergy and there is a craving for more? Has this craving happened to you with alcohol?

13.   Can you safely use alcohol in any form? Did you form the habit? Could you break it? Did you lose your self-confidence? Did you lose your reliance upon things human? Did your problems pile up on you and become difficult to solve?

PARAGRAPH 2

14.   Did frothy emotional appeal (yours or theirs) suffice (work)? Do you believe the message which can interest and hold you must have depth and weight? It needs to be more than emotional, more than intellectual? Do you believe to recreate your life, your ideals must be grounded in a Power greater than yourself?

PARAGRAPH 4

15.   Did you drink for the effect produced by alcohol? Did this effect become so elusive that after a time, even though you knew it was injurious, you could not differentiate the truth from the false?

16.   Did your life seem the only normal one, for you?

17.   Untreated, are you restless, irritable, and discontented? Do you believe that in recovery, you must experience the sense of ease and comfort you get from drinking, and if not, you will drink again and there will be little hope for your recovery unless you experience an entire psychic change?

BIG BOOK PAGE XXIX, PARAGRAPH 1

18.   Do you believe to obtain this psychic change there will be effort necessary and you will have to meet a few requirements and follow a few simple rules?

PARAGRAPH 2

19.   Can you stop on your own? Do you need help?

PARAGRAPH 3

20.   Do you believe that something more than human power is needed to produce the essential psychic change? Is this your only answer?

PARAGRAPH 4

21.   Do you believe your alcoholism is entirely a problem of mental control?

BIG BOOK PAGE XXX, TOP OF PAGE

22.   Has this craving, at times, become more important than all else? Were there times you were not drinking to escape but to overcome a craving beyond your mental control? Were there situations that arose out of this craving that caused you to make a sacrifice rather than to continue to fight?

PARAGRAPH 5

23.   Have you identified your allergy to alcohol as a craving for more alcohol, once you started drinking? Do you believe this allergy differentiates you and sets you apart like a distinct entity? Do you believe the only relief to this physical allergy is entire abstinence? Can you do that on your own?

WEEK 2 – THE DOCTOR'S OPINION

Instructions - The Doctor's Opinion

• BIG BOOK Read - Page xxv, Paragraph 1 to Page xxviii, Paragraph 1
• Read Workbook through the Reading of Normal Person Drinking Alcohol and Abnormal Person Drinking Alcohol.
• Discuss The Disease Concept of Alcoholism Chart (see the next page)
• BIG BOOK Read - Page xxviii, Paragraph 2 to Page xxix, Top of Page
• Workbook Read
• BIG BOOK Read - Page xxix, Paragraph 1 to End of Chapter
• Workbook Read (Summary)
• BIG BOOK Read - Page 355, Paragraph 2 to Page 356, Paragraph 1 (from the personal story, *It Might Have been Worse* - "Study the A.A. book -- don't just read it.")

ASSIGNMENT: Read Chapter 1, "Bill's Story" and mark in the first eight pages what you can relate to as far as Bill's drinking, thinking, and feelings; answer homework questions.

BIG BOOK READ: Page xxv, Paragraph 1 to Page xxviii, Paragraph 1

ALLERGY:

We as laymen have a basic understanding or definition of allergy. I know that if you have an allergy to something, that it would always be indicated or manifested by some physical reaction.

For instance, say you are allergic to strawberries, and you eat them, you will break out in a rash. If you are allergic to penicillin and you take a shot, you'll break out in welts all over your body. Both of those are physical manifestations of an allergy.

When I came to AA, they told me I had an allergy to alcohol, and I could never drink it safely again. How can I have an allergy to alcohol? I drink a quart of vodka a day. How can you drink that much of something you're allergic to? And besides that, it never made me break out in a rash. It doesn't put welts on my body. I didn't understand and I asked them to explain it to me. They said you do not need to understand, all you need to know is that you are allergic to alcohol, and you can't drink. Today I know why they told me that, because they didn't understand it either.

Being an inquisitive alcoholic, I needed to know, and I went to a source which never fails me— the Webster's dictionary. I looked it up and it states: "An allergy is any abnormal reaction to any food, beverage, or substance of any kind." An ABNORMAL REACTION!

I tried to see where I was abnormal when it came to alcohol. To my amazement, I didn't know what was normal or abnormal. For me to find out I had to go to those normal people—the normal social moderate, temperate drinkers. And nine out of ten people are considered to be that way.

I asked if they would describe to me what happens when they take a drink. They said they get a warm comfortable relaxing feeling after one or two drinks. And they don't want any more the rest of the night. I don't feel that way. When I take a drink, I get a "get up and go somewhere and do something" feeling. I don't understand a warm comfortable relaxing feeling. I think it's one of the reasons I loved to drink. It makes me feel different than it does a normal social drinker.

They said something else that absolutely amazed me. When they have two or three drinks, they get a slightly tipsy out of control and the beginnings of a nauseous feeling. They don't like that tipsy nauseous feeling, so therefore they only want one or two drinks. Today I realize that is a normal reaction to alcohol.

Alcohol is a toxic drug. It is a destroyer of human tissue. Normally when you put something in the body that's going to destroy it, the mind and the body will sense what's there and react to that by wanting to regurgitate it up and get it out of there. So, the normal reaction to alcohol is a nauseous feeling, and the body wants to get rid of it.

I don't feel that way; I get an "in-control feeling" when I have a couple. Nor do I get the nauseous feeling in my body. Instead of nausea, my physical reaction is a craving for more of the same. That is a physical craving, and it is so strong that it overcomes the ability of my mind to stop me after I once start. I react entirely abnormally.

The difference between normal and abnormal is that nine out of ten people don't get the physical craving.

We alcoholics react abnormally in two ways: First, it makes us feel different than normal people; and second, it produces the Phenomenon of Craving. That physical craving ensures we will continue till we get drunk, every time we take a drink.

CHRONIC means: "Reacting over and over again."

PHENOMENON means: "Something we do not understand."

CRAVING USUALLY means: "That we are dealing with the mind." But in the context of the Big Book, we are dealing with the body. Craving is what happens after we put one or two drinks in our bodies.

It produces a <u>physical craving</u> for more alcohol.

NORMAL DRINKER

In the normal social drinker—and this is approximately nine people out of ten people—there is a line on that drawing that represents the nine people who can drink safely and are at ease with alcohol. Alcohol is not a problem for them. They take a drink, they put it in their system, the mind and body recognize what it is, the enzyme production begins, and the enzymes begin to attack the alcohol and begin to metabolize or break it down. They break it down to the first state, to a material called acetaldehyde. Then after a time, it's broken down to a material called diacidic acid; then after a period of time, to acetone; and in the final stage it is broken down to a simple carbohydrate which is made up of water, sugar, and carbon dioxide. Now the body can use the sugar. Sugar has calories, it has energy, and the body will store the excess as fat. The water will be dissipated through the urinary and intestinal tracts, the carbon dioxide through the lungs.

In the normal social moderate drinker, the average rate of metabolism of alcohol is one ounce per hour. If the social drinker never drinks more than one ounce per hour, they simply will not get drunk because their body can metabolize it, use it, burn it up, and get rid of excess at that particular rate. That's the normal rate of metabolizing. Very seldom do you see a social drinker drunk. Remember, they get a slightly tipsy, out of control, nauseous feeling and their body will hardly let them get drunk at all.

ABNORMAL DRINKER

This is the one who does not drink safely or who has a dis-ease with alcohol. By the way, that's all the word "disease" means. Something that separates you from a sense of ease, something that separates you from the normal things that happen to most people. When we alcoholics put a drink in our bodies, the same thing starts to take place. The mind and body recognize what it is, and the enzyme production starts to attack the alcohol and break it down first to acetaldehyde. Then to diacidic acid, then after a period of time to acetone. Now it seems as though in the body of the alcoholic, the enzymes necessary to break it down from acetone to the simple carbohydrates are not there in the same qualities and quantities as in the body of the non-alcoholic. Therefore, the enzymes necessary to break it down from acetone to the simple carbohydrates are not there, so the breakdown rate is a slower operation. For the alcoholic, we break it down at the rate of 3/4 ounce per hour or 1/2 ounce per hour, maybe 1/4 ounce, maybe 1/5 depending on the enzyme production and the stage of alcoholism we're in.

The medical profession today has proven beyond any shadow of a doubt that acetone ingested into the human system, which remains there for an appreciable period of time, will produce an actual physical craving for more of the same. As that craving is produced for more of the same, then the body begins to say to the mind, "Let me have more of that stuff you just put in there." So instead of having the one or two drinks we intended to have, the body says, "Give me the second drink, the third drink until I am drunk." Now the first drink was caused by the mind. The drinks after that were caused by the craving in the body.

I think that one of the most interesting things that they have come up with recently is this: the medical profession has proven that acetone ingested into the human system over a period of time is an actual destroyer of human tissue. As we drink more and more, we destroy more and more human tissue in all parts of the body. But it seems as though the first two organs of the body that are attacked in most cases are the liver and the pancreas. They have also proven today that the enzymes necessary to metabolize alcohol come from the liver and the pancreas. As we drink, and we begin to damage the organs of the body, the enzyme production becomes less and less, and the phenomenon of craving becomes stronger and stronger.

As you can see, you and I not only have a disease, we have a progressive disease guaranteed to get worse as time goes by because we are destroying the organs of the body that are necessary to metabolize alcohol. We know also that as we grow older, everything that the body produces begins to shut down. As we get older, the enzyme production becomes less due to the aging factor. Our disease is a progressive disease whether we drink or not. The fact that we are allergic to alcohol is academic if we don't take the first drink. We need to understand that, because the main problem and the solution are going to be within the mind, even though the body is going to get worse with age. I think sometimes in AA we do not explain to the new people about the physical factor of their disease.

In the era the Big Book was written, medical science had not yet uncovered the chemical breakdown that occurs in the body.

That is why Dr. Silkworth called it a Phenomenon of Craving. Today science and the AMA have discovered the exact physical reaction that takes place when we ingest alcohol into our system.

Leader will explain the disease concept of alcoholism as illustrated in the chart on the following page.

The Disease Concept of Alcoholism
(The Doctor's Opinion)

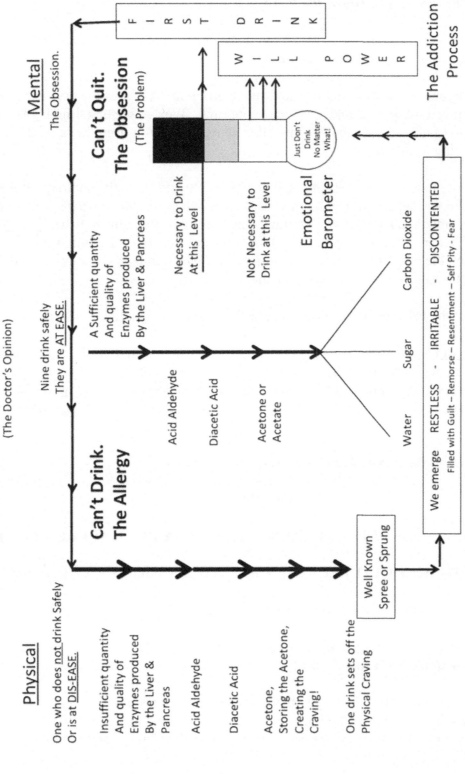

Physical

One who does not drink Safely
Or is at DIS-EASE.

Insufficient quantity
And quality of
Enzymes produced
By the Liver &
Pancreas

Acid Aldehyde

Diacetic Acid

Acetone,
Storing the Acetone,
Creating the
Craving!

One drink sets off the
Physical Craving

Well Known
Spree or Sprung

Mental

The Obsession.

Nine drink safely
They are AT EASE.

Can't Quit.
The Obsession
(The Problem)

Can't Drink.
The Allergy

A Sufficient quantity
And quality of
Enzymes produced
By the Liver & Pancreas

Acid Aldehyde

Diacetic Acid

Acetone or
Acetate

Necessary to Drink
At this Level

Not Necessary to
Drink at this Level

Just Don't
Drink
No Matter
What!

Emotional
Barometer

F		D
I		R
R		I
S		N
T		K

W		P
I		O
L		W
L		E
		R

Water   Sugar   Carbon Dioxide

We emerge   RESTLESS - IRRITABLE - DISCONTENTED
Filled with Guilt – Remorse – Resentment – Self Pity - Fear

"Powerless Over Alcohol"

**The Addiction
Process**

27

BIG BOOK Read Page xxviii, Paragraph 2
READ AFTER: Page xxix, Top of the Page

We must understand if we are going to deal with alcoholics, that practicing alcoholics <u>cannot differentiate the truth from the false</u>. To most of them, what they are doing is absolutely normal. It is all the normal people who are abnormal. We surround ourselves with people of our own kind. Deluding our minds into thinking that we are different. As far as the practicing alcoholic is concerned, it is the normal drinkers who are abnormal. We can see that drinking is injurious and gets us into trouble, but we really cannot differentiate the truth from the false, because to us what we are doing is normal.

An obsession of the mind is an idea that overcomes all other ideas to the contrary. It is so strong that it will make you believe something that isn't true. When we drank, we had a couple of drinks and they made us feel better. Our minds tied those two thoughts together. <u>Feel bad, take a drink and feel better</u>. That is a mental addiction, not a physical one. The mind says it's okay to take a drink and the mind really believes that it's okay. The mind says, this time it will be different, and the mind believes it. That is believing a lie!

Any alcoholic who believes he can drink successfully is believing a lie.

The <u>obsession of the mind</u> causes us to believe a lie and take that first drink. As soon as we put the first drink in our body, the allergy takes over and we cannot stop. The one thing that you and I can do for the practicing alcoholic is to help them see the <u>allergy of the body</u> and the <u>obsession of the mind</u> that they are experiencing. I didn't know about these two problems when I was drinking.

BIG BOOK Read Page xxix, *Paragraph 1 to End of Chapter*

SUMMARY:

IF YOU CAN'T DRINK BECAUSE OF THE PHYSICAL ALERGY BODY,

AND CAN'T QUIT BECAUSE OF THE OBSESSION OF THE MIND,

THEN YOU ARE PROBABLY POWERLESS OVER ALCOHOL.

BIG BOOK: Page 355, Paragraph 2 to Page 356, Paragraph 2
"Study the AA Book don't just read it!"

Read Chapter 1, "Bill's Story." As you read the first eight pages of Bill's Story, mark what you can relate to as far as <u>drinking, thinking, and feeling</u>. Continue to write how you are powerless over alcohol, your history and reservations, and how your ideas have changed as a result of reading the Doctor's Opinion and Bill's Story.

ASSIGNMENT: Answer homework questions for "Bill's Story"

BILL'S STORY QUESTIONS

PAGE 1

1.   Did alcohol work for you?

2.   Did it affect the way you thought and felt?

PAGE 3

3.   Did alcohol take an important and exhilarating part of your life?

4.   Did your drinking later assume more serious proportions?

PAGE 5

5.   Did you ever ask: "Was I crazy?"

6.   Did alcohol cease to be a luxury and become a necessity?

7.   Did things gradually get worse?

8.   Do you still think you could control it? (Alcohol or the situations your life?)

PAGE 6

9.   Did you ever feel the remorse, horror, and hopelessness of the next morning?

10.   Did your mind ever race uncontrollably?

11.   Did you ever seek oblivion?

PAGE 7

12.   Can self-knowledge fix you?

PAGE 8

13.   Did you ever feel lonely?

14.   Did you feel fear?

15.   Can fear keep you sober?

16.   Were you overwhelmed by alcohol?

17.   Was alcohol your master?

PAGE 10

18.   What was your reaction to religion, the church, and God? (Share this with your sponsor or close AA friends.)

PAGE 12

Note what happened to Bill's prejudice against "their God" when he began to apply his own concept of God.

19.   Did you know that "nothing more was required of me to make my beginning" than willingness or a willingness to believe?

PAGE 13

20.   Can you admit for the first time that of yourself you are nothing, and without God you are lost?

21.   Does Bill essentially take the First through the Eleventh Step at this time?

WEEK 3 – BILL'S STORY

Instructions - Bill's Story

• BIG BOOK Read - Page 1, Paragraph 1 to Page 8, Paragraph 3
• Workbook Read
• BIG BOOK Read - Page 8, Paragraph 4 to Page 9, Paragraph 5
• Workbook Read
• BIG BOOK Read - Page 9, Paragraph 6 to Page 13, Top of Page
• Workbook Read
• BIG BOOK Read - Page 13, Paragraph 1 to End of Chapter
• Workbook Read

ASSIGNMENT: Read Chapter 2, "There is a Solution," and answer homework questions.

BIG BOOK READ: *Page 1, Paragraph 1 to Page 8, Paragraph 3*

Bill put together a business deal on the condition that he would not drink. He would have shared generously in the profits. But that evening in a hotel room, one of the men passed a bottle of applejack around. It went by Bill the first time, he said, "No thank you, I'm not drinking." The next time it came by his mind told him that one little drink of applejack wouldn't hurt. He took a drink and that triggered the allergy, and he could not stop blowing the whole deal. The importance of that statement is in the next paragraph. For the first time, he could see what alcohol was doing to him. <u>He could differentiate the truth from the false.</u>

People call us weak-willed people; we are not weak-willed people. The problem is, we are strong-willed people. **Our will is so strong**, we almost killed ourselves from drinking alcohol. We almost killed ourselves trying to find a way to drink and not get drunk. Weak-willed people do not become alcoholics. The third time they vomit they quit drinking. Us alkies literally kill ourselves trying to find a way to drink.

BIG BOOK READ: *Page 8, Paragraph 4, Page 9, Paragraph 5*

The friend that came to see Bill was Ebby Thatcher. Ebby and Bill were old school friends. They drank together on many occasions. Bill heard that Ebby had gotten into a lot of trouble. Ebby came from a great family, but they had a lot of trouble with him. Ebby's father had passed away and had given Ebby his summer home. Ebby was supposed to be fixing it up. His family always kept Ebby somewhere else. You know the family that will always help you— if you stay over there. They were trying to get rid of Ebby up there in this little house.

31

He was supposed to be painting it and fixing it up to live in. When he was painting it, he had painted one side, and the pigeons shit all over it. He got a shotgun and shot the pigeons off the roof. Ebby set it on fire one time, drunk. Then he ran a car into a lady's house one day, drunk. They had him up before the judge, and they were going to put him into the nut house. In those days they didn't have treatment centers, so they put you in the state hospital. Bill had not heard about this. This is what Bill meant by "recapturing the spirit of other days."

BIG BOOK READ: Page 9, Paragraph 6, to Page 13, Paragraph to the Top of Page

What Ebby really told Bill was about Rowland Hazard and another guy who appeared in court and persuaded the judge to suspend his commitment for Ebby and turn him loose into their custody. They said, we believe we have found a way that Ebby can live without drinking. The judges then were like they are today; they really don't want to put us in nut houses and prisons, and if they can avoid it, they do what they can. The judge turned him loose in Rowland's care.

Rowland took Ebby home for a couple of weeks and got him into the Oxford Groups. Then he took him down to New York City, and there Ebby went to work for Sam Shoemaker in the Bowery Mission. He was attending Oxford Group meetings and he heard about his friend Bill, so he went to see Bill. I believe this was the first Twelfth Step call on an alcoholic.

He told Bill how these two guys had appeared in front of the judge. He said "Bill, they took me to the Oxford Groups. There I learned that the answer and the solution to our problem is a Power greater than human power, a vital spiritual experience."

For the first time, Bill not only understood the problem (information that he got from Dr. Silkworth) but now he could see the solution to the problem. Ebby brought to Bill what later turned out to be Step Two. Then he laid out for him a Practical Program of Action. He said, "Bill, if you will follow this program of action, you will find that Power greater than you and you won't have to drink. That is what I've been doing, and I've been sober for two months."

Ebby laid out for Bill the Practical Program of Action, which later turned out to be Steps Three through Twelve. Now we see that Bill had access to the first three Steps. We saw him take Step One when he admitted he was powerless. There was no Step One written in those days, but we could see that he made that admission. For the first time, Bill knew all three things.

The Problem, The Solution, & The Practical Program of Action!

BIG BOOK READ: Page 13, Paragraph 1, To The End

Now we are going to find as we go through the Big Book that Bill, like so many writers, builds in your mind by painting pictures with the use of words. He's going to be talking all the way through the Book about a **wonderful, effective, spiritual structure**. Later, he's going to tell us what that structure is, and we are going to pass through it to freedom. That last statement is his first reference to this.

He said, upon a foundation of complete willingness I might build what I saw in my friend. The foundation of our recovery is based on willingness and that really comes through Step One, where we admit we are powerless over alcohol. If we can make that admission 100% then we can begin to believe in a Power greater than ourselves.

Until we can make that admission, we and alcohol are the power greater than ourselves. Our real growth and spiritual structure will start with Step One, willingness, which is the foundation. Then later we are going to see where believing Step Two becomes the cornerstone of the spiritual structure.

Bill has now taken Steps One and Two, although no Steps were written in those days. We can see Bill doing those two things, the admission of powerlessness and the coming to believe.

The Big Book was originated in textbook form as a Twelfth Step call, to reach people who weren't in Akron or New York. Anyone who picked up a copy of it could read and identify with the Book. So, Bill's Story fits in here exactly where it should in the standard textbook theory and as a Twelfth Step call for the new person.

I can almost see him as he finishes up this chapter—I've described the vital spiritual experience and it's going to seem to many of them like some great happening way out there in the sky. It probably sounds a lot like religion and theology. He said, "Maybe I had better get down to brass tacks and tell them exactly what took place in my life."

In the next chapter, "There Is a Solution," he tells us exactly how this happened. Remember in the beginning there was Bill and Ebby, that was the fellowship. Ebby brought to Bill the answer and the solution to our problem. Bill applied them and recovered through a vital spiritual experience. So, two things had to take place here: first the fellowship with Ebby, then the vital spiritual experience. And as the result of this course of action, Bill also got sober. The next chapter explains exactly what these two things are all about.

Read Chapter 2. There is a solution. Start writing what you can truly "manage" in your life. As thoughts occur to you about whether you can or cannot manage life alone and in particular your life, write down your thoughts in your notebook.

ASSIGNMENT: Answer questions for "There Is a Solution"

THERE IS A SOLUTION QUESTIONS

PAGE 17

1.   Is the Fellowship by itself enough for you?

2.   Do you, on your own, without help, have a way out?

PAGE 18

3.   Have you come to believe you suffer from an illness?

4.   Did it engulf all whose lives touched you?

5.   Did you see how you can reach another alcoholic?

PAGE 19

6.   Is the elimination of your drinking enough or only a beginning?

7.   If you go on just not drinking, will the problem be taken care of?

PAGE 20

8.   Does your life depend upon your constant thought of others and how you may help meet their needs?

9.   Are you curious to discover how and why these people have recovered from a hopeless state of mind and body?

10.   The Big Book answers the question, "what do I have to do?" Have you asked yourself that question?

11.   Can you take alcohol or leave it alone?

PAGE 21

12.   Did you have the habit badly enough to gradually impair you physically and mentally?

13.   If given a good reason, can you give up alcohol?

14.   From your examination of yourself in the past weeks and your reading of the Big Book, are you a "real alcoholic?" If not, why not?

15.   Did you at some stage of your drinking lose control of the amount once you started to drink?

16.   Did you lose control, did you do absurd things, were you a Dr. Jekyll and Mr. Hyde?

These questions and observations on Page 21 may help you in answering the question you have been writing about, having to do with your powerlessness over alcohol.

PAGE 23

17.   Can you control the amount of alcohol once you start?

18.   Does your experience abundantly confirm that once you put any alcohol into your system, something happens which makes it virtually impossible for you to stop?

19.   Have you discovered your own truth about alcohol?

20.   Are these observations important to know and pointless if you never take the first drink?

21.   Therefore, do you believe that the main problem centers in your mind rather than in your body?

22.   Did this malady of the mind have a real hold on you and were you baffled?

23.   Have you suffered from the obsession that somehow, someday, you will beat the game?

24.   Have you lost control? Do you believe you can assert your willpower to stay stopped?

This sums up our common problem that is covered so far as to the admission of powerlessness over alcohol, physically, after we start.

PAGE 24

25.   At a certain point in your drinking, did you pass into a state where the most powerful desire to stop drinking was of absolutely no avail?

26.   Is it a fact that you have lost the power of choice in drink?

27.   Has your so-called "willpower" become practically nonexistent and were you unable at certain times to bring into your consciousness with sufficient force the memory of the suffering and humiliation of even a week or a month ago?

28.   Are you without defense against the first drink?

29.   When thoughts of the consequences of your drinking occurred, was thinking it through enough for you?

30.   Have you said to yourself, "It won't hurt me this time"? And were there times you didn't think at all?

31.   Has this sort of thinking fully established itself in you and have you placed yourself beyond human aid?

PAGE 25

32.   Do you believe the process requires self-searching, the leveling of our pride, and the confession of shortcomings for a successful consummation?

33. Do you believe there is anything less for you than a deep and effective spiritual experience that will revolutionize your attitude toward life, your fellows, and God's universe?

34. Do you believe there is any middle-of-the-road solution for you?

35. Were you in a position where life was becoming impossible, and you had passed into the region from which there was no return through human aid?

36. Do you have any other alternatives but to go on to the bitter end, blotting out the consciousness of your intolerable situation as best you can or accept spiritual help?

PAGE 26

37. Do you honestly want to accept spiritual help and are you willing to make the effort?

38. Do you believe that with a profound knowledge of the inner workings of your mind, relapse is unthinkable?

PAGE 29

39. In the mental sense (before the first drink) am I one of these people and must I have this thing?

WEEK 4 - THERE IS A SOLUTION

Instructions - There Is A Solution

• BIG BOOK Read - Page 17, Paragraphs 1 and 2
• Workbook Read
• BIG BOOK Read - Page 17, Paragraph 3
• Workbook Read
• BIG BOOK Read - Page 18, Paragraph 1 to Page 23, Paragraph 2
• Workbook Read
• BIG BOOK Read - Page 23, Paragraph 3 to Page 25, Top of Page
• Workbook Read
• BIG BOOK Read - Page 567, Appendix II (back of book)
• BIG BOOK Read - Page 25, Paragraph 1 to Page 26, Top of Page
• Workbook Read
• Discuss "What Is the Solution Chart"
• BIG BOOK Read - Page 26, Paragraph 1 to Page 28, Top of Page
• Workbook Read
• BIG BOOK Read - Page 28, Paragraph 1 to End of Chapter
• Workbook Read

ASSIGNMENT: Read Chapter 3, "More about Alcoholism" and answer homework questions.

BIG BOOK READ: Page 17, Paragraphs 1 and 2

We think that in and of itself the Fellowship would never have held us together as we are now joined; this is an important warning in the Book. The Fellowship of Alcoholics Anonymous is a great thing; there is a lot of power in people supporting each other. The Fellowship is a strong support group. It is very therapeutic to be among other people who have recovered from the same problem as you.

Earlier on, people in this program didn't have a lot of problems like we have today with the Fellowship. The earlier people didn't have a lot of Fellowship; there were just a few little groups when this Book was written. A group in New York and the rest of them in Cleveland, Akron, and scattered around here and there. So, you see, they could not go to 90 meetings in 90 days. They had to work the real program out of the Big Book.

Now that we have so much Fellowship, you can just go around Fellowshipping and never work the program in the Book. You can just live off the Fellowship, but you cannot get sober off the Fellowship alone, because the vital spiritual experience comes from the action outlined in the first

164 pages of the Big Book. The Fellowship will not change your life. Some people say go to 90 meetings in 90 days and you will get sober. You may get dry from alcohol, but you don't recover from the dis-ease. You can no more get sober doing that than you can become a parent by going to 90 PTA meetings in 90 days. You must take some other steps.

BIG BOOK READ: Page 17, Paragraph 3

Bill is saying Fellowship is not enough. He said, "The tremendous fact for every one of us is that we have discovered a common solution." The common problem is a great bond, but he said the real thing is this common solution. This Book carries the great message of the common solution. Later, it is going to tell us that the common solution to alcoholism is a vital spiritual experience.

We have already determined in the first part of the Book that we are powerless. In this part of the Book, he writes the prescription. The prescription is power, and he says the power of the Fellowship and the power of the common solution will overcome any person's powerlessness over alcohol.

Anyone can get sober, but the real question is, how do you stay sober? How do you change? How do you learn to live in such a manner that you will be able to stay sober in the future?

And he warns us, that even though the Fellowship is one of the powerful elements in the cement that binds us together, that the Fellowship alone is not enough. The great fact is that we need both elements for recovery. Which are the same two things he had to have to recover—the Fellowship he had with Ebby, and the practical program of action, which lead him to the vital spiritual experience, which in turn, is the real solution to the disease of alcoholism.

BIG BOOK READ: Page 18, Paragraph 1 to Page 23, Paragraph 2

There is no way that I can trigger my allergy, produce the phenomenon of craving, end up drunk, sick, and in trouble, if I don't take the first drink. That makes good sense to me. The fact that I am allergic to alcohol is important for me to understand, but the real problem centers in the mind rather than the body. All action is born in thought! There is no way that I can drink unless my mind tells me that it's okay to take a drink.

"There is the obsession that somehow, someday, we will beat the game." Here is the word "obsession" now entering into the picture. The great obsession of every alcoholic is to drink like normal people. This is the great lie that we believe: that someday, somehow, we are going to be able to beat the game. We believe a lie and, based on the lie, we decide to take a drink. We take the drink and that triggers the allergy and then we cannot stop drinking. The real problem centers in the mind rather than the body.

BIG BOOK READ: Page 23, Paragraph 3 to Page 25, Top of Page

"We are without defense against the first drink." If we could remember what a drink does to us, if only we could remember the jail houses, the divorce courts, the hospitals, the humiliations and pain and sufferings of the last drunk—we wouldn't take a drink. But we can't remember with sufficient force to keep us from taking the first drink. The mind will give us some excuse to take it.

"There is a complete failure of the kind of defense that keeps one from putting his hand on a hot stove." Alcohol is a lot like a hot stove, it has burned us over and over again. We are strangely insane when it comes to alcohol.

If we have placed ourselves "beyond human aid," then the Fellowship of Alcoholics Anonymous alone will not bring about recovery from the disease of alcoholism because the Fellowship is made up of a bunch of human beings who are just as powerless as I am. Recovery will have to come through something other than human power.

BIG BOOK READ: Page 567, Spiritual Experience, Appendix II
BIG BOOK READ: Page 25, Paragraph 1 to Page 26, Top of Page

I have learned a couple of things by reading this appendix. My conception of a spiritual experience is not at all what I had when I first read the Book. This is an entirely different conception. I have learned that it doesn't make any difference whether it is a spiritual experience or a spiritual awakening, either one can occur. One is fast and one is slow, but the end result will be that I've tapped an unsuspected inner resource of strength, which I will identify as a Power greater than human power, or God as I understand Him. This is a key statement that we need to remember, because later we are going to be looking at this unsuspected inner resource of strength.

The key word in this whole appendix is change. Bill is the kind of writer who repeats himself over and over. A good writer will use a different word to repeat himself. If you'll notice on Page 567, he uses the word change in many ways. In the first paragraph, he talked about a personality change sufficient to recover. In the second paragraph, he again said personality changes, but then he said in the nature of sudden and spectacular upheavals; an upheaval is a change. In the third paragraph he talks about a number of sudden revolutionary changes; to revolutionize is to change something entirely. Also, in the third paragraph he talks about immediate and overwhelming God consciousness; to overwhelm something is to change it. We have a vast change in feeling and outlook.

In the fourth paragraph, the first sentence, he talks about transformations; to transform is to change. In the middle of the paragraph, he talks about profound alterations; to alter is to change. The key idea in this vital spiritual experience is to change our personality.

When we get to AA, we are usually restless, irritable, and discontent. We come in filled with shame, fear, guilt, and remorse. That is our personality when we enter AA. If we want to stay sober, we are going to need to find a way to live. We are going to change our personalities, become peaceful, happy, serene, useful, helpful human beings. The Fellowship alone will not bring that change in us without the Practical Program of Action that is outlined in the first 164 pages. The combination of both will bring about this vital spiritual experience

We have been told in the Book that there are two powers. One is the Fellowship and the other is in this common solution, which is the Practical Program of Action, which will give us the vital spiritual experience. We need both powers in order to recover. I doubt if any of us are going to recover without the Fellowship. I also doubt if any of us will recover without the vital spiritual experience.

The only two alternatives we have are: First, to go on to the bitter end, blotting out the consciousness of our intolerable situation as best we can; and second, to believe and accept spiritual help.

A good textbook never tells you something without giving you a good example of it. The Doctor's Opinion was followed up by Bill's Story, in which lies the perfect example of alcoholism. He has now told us of the need for the vital spiritual experience. On Page 26 we see an example of a fellow who had this vital spiritual experience and where the idea came from, his name is Rowland Hazard. He is the man that went to the judge and got Ebby Thatcher released into his custody.

Discuss What Is the Solution? Chart

BIG BOOK READ: Page 26, Paragraph 1 to Page 28, Top of Page

Dr. Carl Jung, a celebrated psychiatrist, gave Rowland the solution, a vital spiritual experience. Rowland came back to New York and got involved in the Oxford Group program. By using their steps and their planned program of action, he was able to find God's Power and recover.

Now we can see where the Steps came from, Step One came from Doctor Silkworth, a non-alcoholic; Step Two came from Dr. Carl Jung, another non-alcoholic. Rowland got in the Oxford Group, another group of non-alcoholics. The strange thing is how God used all these people to put this program together. Bill was the key figure to put all these ideas into our program of action, but Bill did not create any of these Steps. Bill's mind was used by God as a vessel to put all these ideas together, to bring us the program we know today.

BIG BOOK READ: Page 28, Paragraph 1 to Page 29, End of Chapter

"Further on, clear-cut directions are given showing how we recovered." We have seen the words "precise" and "specific," and now we see the words "clear-cut." This does not sound like cafeteria-style to us, it does not sound like take what you want and leave the rest. They are telling us exactly what they have had to do to recover from the disease of alcoholism. The things we have learned up to this point are the things they had to learn in order to recover.

Has your writing in your notebook listed those things you attempted to do to control your use of alcohol and your failures? Be prepared to discuss how it applies in your life with your sponsor.

ASSIGNMENT: Read Chapter 3, "More About Alcoholism"; Answer homework questions for "More About Alcoholism".

What Is The Solution?

The Fellowship as it existed in 1939

The Fellowship Supports Us

Spiritual Experience or Spiritual Awakening That Changes Us

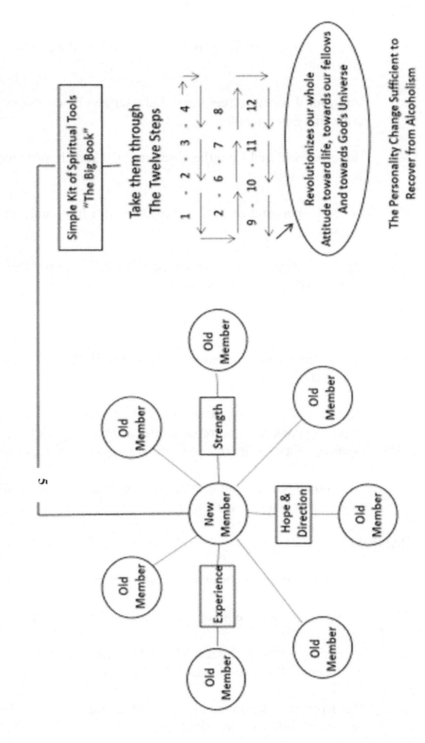

Simple Kit of Spiritual Tools "The Big Book"

Take them through The Twelve Steps

1 - 2 - 3 - 4
2 - 6 - 7 - 8
9 - 10 - 11 - 12

Revolutionizes our whole Attitude toward life, towards our fellows And towards God's Universe

The Personality Change Sufficient to Recover from Alcoholism

Old Member

Strength

New Member

Hope & Direction

Experience

Old Member

Old Member

Old Member

Old Member

Old Member

5

41

MORE ABOUT ALCOHOLISM QUESTIONS

PAGE 30

1.   Have you been unwilling to admit you are a real alcoholic and are you bodily and mentally different?

2.   Has your drinking career been characterized by countless vain attempts to prove you can drink like other people?

3.   Have you suffered from the obsession that somehow, someday, you can control and enjoy your drinking?

4.   Was the persistence of this illusion astonishing and did you pursue it into the gates of insanity?

5.   Have you learned that you must fully concede to your innermost self that you are an alcoholic?

6.   Is this the first step in recovery?

7.   Do you believe the delusion that you are like other people or presently may be has to be smashed?

8.   Do you believe that you will ever recover control? And did you at times feel you were regaining control but were such intervals usually brief and inevitably followed by still less control, which led in time to pitiful and incomprehensible demoralization?

9.   Are you convinced you were in the grip of a progressive illness and over any considerable time you get worse, never better?

PAGE 31

10.   Does there appear to be any kind of treatment that will make you like other people?

11.   Do you believe there is such a thing as making a normal drinker out of an alcoholic?

12.   By every form of self-deception and experimentation, have you tried to prove yourself an exception to the rule, therefore nonalcoholic?

13.   Have you tried long enough and hard enough to drink like other people? What are some of the methods you have tried?

PAGE 32

14.   To get a full knowledge of your condition (if there were no other way to find out) would you be willing to consider the idea of diagnosing yourself and trying some controlled drinking? Trying to drink and stopping abruptly, trying it more than once?

15.   Do you believe that a long period of sobriety and self-discipline would qualify you to drink like other people?

16.   Do you believe that by gathering all your forces, you could stop altogether?

PAGE 33

17.   Do you believe to stop drinking there must be no reservations of any kind, or any lurking notion that someday you will be immune to alcohol?

18.   Can you stay stopped on your own willpower?

PAGE 34

19.   Do you desire to stop altogether, and can you do that on a non-spiritual basis? Have you lost the power to choose whether you will drink or not drink?

20.   No matter how great the necessity or wish, can you leave it alone (stay stopped)?

PAGE 35

21.   Do you believe that the crux of your problem is the mental state which would precede a relapse into drinking?

22.   Do you believe that if you fail to enlarge your spiritual life, you will drink again?

PAGE 37

23.   During your drinking, did your sound thinking fail to hold you in check, and did an insane idea win out?

PAGE 38

24.   However intelligent you may have been in other respects, where alcohol is involved, are you strangely insane?

PAGE 39

25. Do you believe you could stay stopped based on self-knowledge alone?

PAGE 42

26. Do you have an alcoholic mind? Do you believe that the time and place will come that you will drink again?

27. Do you believe this problem has you hopelessly defeated? Has this process snuffed out the last flicker of conviction that you can do the job yourself?

28. Do you believe that you will have to throw several lifelong conceptions out the window to go through with the program of action?

29. Have you discovered that spiritual principles will solve all your problems?

PAGE 43

30. Is there any doubt in your mind that you are 100% hopeless apart from divine help and is there any other solution?

31. Do you believe that at certain times you will have no effective mental defense against the first drink and that neither you nor any other human being can provide that defense? Must your defense come from a Higher Power?

Instructions - More About Alcoholism

• Workbook Read
• BIG BOOK Read - Page 30, Paragraphs 1 and 2
• Workbook Read
• BIG BOOK Read - Page 30, Paragraph 3 to Page 43, End of Chapter
• Workbook Read

ASSIGNMENT: Read Chapter 4, "We Agnostics" and answer homework questions.

Bill said, "Even though I've told them of the need for spirituality, they still are not going to want it. They have the same aversions to spirituality and religion as I had. I should explain to them a little more about the disease in order to convince them of the need for the vital spiritual experience."

In this chapter, "More about Alcoholism," he shows us why we are going to need to have a spiritual awakening if we are going to recover. In this chapter, he talks about one thing and one thing only: the <u>Insanity of Alcoholism</u>.

BIG BOOK READ: Page 30, Paragraph 1 and 2, to Page 30, Paragraph 2

Many of us in AA have been very confused about the word insanity. Many of us said, "I didn't have any trouble with that word because I remember all the crazy stupid things I did while drinking." Those crazy stupid things we did while we were drinking were not caused by insanity, they were caused by alcohol. It is a sedative drug that lowers your inhibitions and allows you to do stupid crazy things.

Insanity deals with the <u>inability to see the truth</u>. It has nothing to do with being crazy. If you are a crazy person, that means you've lost most of your brains. Insanity is entirely different than crazy. It deals with the <u>ability to see the truth</u> about a subject or not see it. In the dictionary, the word sane means "<u>a whole mind</u>." If you are sane, your mind is whole, and you can see the truth. If you are insane, your mind is less than whole. At certain times you can't see the truth about something. It does not mean you are all gone, it just means that you are not quite all here. And when it comes to alcohol, at times we are not quite all here.

We seem to be unable to see the truth, we believe a lie about alcohol. If you believe a lie, your mind is less than whole, and you have a degree of insanity. That's all we are referring to when we talk about insanity. Bill used three words meaning the same thing: obsession, illusion, and delusion. They all mean believing a lie.

The rest of this chapter is devoted to examples that show us believing a lie. The state of the mind just prior to taking the first drink. Now, remember that just prior to taking the first drink the mind is stone-cold sober. Let's look at the mind, alcohol-free, just prior to the first drink.

BIG BOOK READ: Page 30, Paragraph 3, to Page 43, End of Chapter

Bill has convinced me in this chapter that if I don't have that vital spiritual awakening, there is no way I will stay sober because my insanity will always lead me back to thinking I can take that first drink.

Now we are faced with the idea that we are going to need a vital spiritual experience. Coming from a religion that taught me hellfire and brimstone put me in a terrible spot. Thank God Bill came from the same place. Knowing that it was vital to our recovery, he wrote us another chapter, "We Agnostics."

I think "We Agnostics" is the greatest piece of spiritual information I have ever read. AA has given me two things; it gives me the concept of God as I understand Him. But Chapter 4 gives me a new understanding of God. It's in Chapter 4 that my God changed from hellfire and brimstone to a kind and loving God. Chapter 4 lets me make that leap from what God used to be, to a person who can use God in his life and have that vital spiritual experience.

I am going to have to decide soon. I'll have to decide to continue drinking till I die or live on a spiritual basis. Based on my own knowledge, I cannot make that decision. Thank God for Chapter 4.

By now you should have completed writing most of your memories about why you are powerless over alcohol and why your life is unmanageable. If you are having difficulty with these problems, discuss this with your sponsor or spiritual advisor.

ASSIGNMENT: Read Chapter 4, answer homework questions for "We Agnostics "

WE AGNOSTICS QUESTIONS

PAGE 44

1.   Does a spiritual experience seem impossible? Do you feel you are an atheist? Are you an agnostic?

2.   Have you had to face the fact that you must find a spiritual basis of life or else?

PAGE 45

3.   Would a mere code of morals or a better philosophy of life be sufficient to overcome your alcoholism?

4.   Is lack of power your dilemma?

5.   Do you believe the main object of this Book is to enable you to find a Power greater than yourself, which will solve your problem?

PAGE 46

6.   When God is mentioned, do you have honest doubt and prejudice?

7.   Have you been able to lay aside prejudice and express a willingness to believe in a Power greater than yourself?

8.   Do you believe your own conception, however inadequate, is sufficient to make an approach and to affect a contact with God (provided you take other simple steps)?

9.   Do you believe the realm of the spirit is broad, roomy, and all-inclusive?

PAGE 47

10.   Do you believe this is all you need to commence spiritual growth and to effect your first conscious relation with God? (First half of Step Two.)

11.   Do you now believe or are you even willing to believe that there is a Power greater than yourself? Do you believe that upon this simple cornerstone, a wonderfully effective spiritual structure can be built?

12.   Do you believe you cannot make use of spiritual principles unless you accept many things on faith that seem difficult to believe (do you believe there is a process from simple belief to faith)?

PAGE 48

13.   Have you found yourself handicapped by obstinacy, sensitiveness, and unreasoning prejudice, and has even casual reference to spiritual things make you bristle with antagonism? Do you believe this thinking has to be abandoned?

14.   Faced with alcoholism destruction (Step One) have you become as open-minded on spiritual matters as you tried to be on other questions? In this respect, was alcohol a great persuader? Did it finally beat you into a state of reasonableness?

PAGE 49

15.   In the past have you chosen to believe that your human intelligence was the last word, the alpha and the omega, the beginning and the end of all? Was that vain of you?

PAGE 50

16.   Have you ever given the spiritual side of life a fair hearing?

17.   Do you believe you need to gain access to and belief in a Power greater than yourself? Do you believe that this Power, in your case, can accomplish the miraculous, the humanly impossible?

18.   Do you believe you will have to wholeheartedly meet a few simple requirements to have a revolutionary change in your way of living and thinking?

PAGE 51

19.   Leaving aside the drink question, do you see the underlying reasons why you were making heavy going of life (Lack of Power)?

20.   In the realm of the spirit, has your mind been fettered by superstition, tradition, and all sorts of fixed ideas?

PAGE 52

21.   Do you need to ask yourself, why you should apply to your human problems (the unmanageability of your life) the same readiness to change your point of view?

22.   Did you stop doubting the power of God when you saw others solve their problems by a simple reliance upon God?

23.   In the past, have you stuck to the idea that self-sufficiency will solve your problems?

PAGE 53

24. Do you believe it is saner and more logical to believe than not to believe?

25. Faced with Step One, crushed by a self-imposed crisis that you cannot postpone or evade, do you believe you have to fearlessly face the proposition that either <u>God is everything or else He is nothing</u>? That <u>God either is or He isn't</u>? What is your choice to be (second half of Step Two)?

26. Arrived at this point, are you squarely confronted with the question of faith? Can you duck the issue? Have you already walked far <u>over the bridge of reason</u> toward the desired shore of faith?

27. Have you been <u>faithful to the god of reason</u>, so in one way or another, have you discovered that faith has been involved all the time?

PAGE 54

28. Can you still say the whole thing is nothing, created out of nothing, meaning nothing?

29. Have you seen that reason isn't everything?

PAGE 55

30. Have you been fooling yourself? Do you believe deep down within every man, woman, and child is the fundamental idea of God?

31. Have you seen that faith in some sort of God is a part of your make-up? Just as much as the feeling you have for a friend?

32. Do you believe He is as much a fact as you are?
Do you believe you will find the great reality deep down within?
Do you believe in the last analysis, it is ONLY there (Deep Down Within) that God can be found?

33. Has the testimony of these people helped to sweep away prejudice, enabled you to think honestly, encouraged you to search diligently within yourself, and do you believe with this <u>attitude</u> you cannot fail? Do you believe that the consciousness of your belief will surely come to you?

34. Do you believe as you draw near to God, He will disclose Himself to you?

Instructions - We Agnostics

• BIG BOOK Read - Page 44, Paragraphs 1 to 3
• Workbook Read
• BIG BOOK Read - Page 44, Paragraph 4 to Page 45, Paragraph 2
• Workbook Read
• BIG BOOK Read - Page 45, Paragraph 3 to Page 47, Paragraph 2
• Workbook Read
• BIG BOOK Read - Page 47, Paragraph 3 to Page 48, Paragraph 1
• Workbook Read
• BIG BOOK Read - Page 48, Paragraph 3 to Page 51, Paragraph 1
• Workbook Read
• BIG BOOK Read - Page 51, Paragraph 2 to Page 55, Top of Page
• Workbook Read
• BIG BOOK Read - Page 55, Paragraph 1 to Page 57, End of Chapter
• Workbook Read

ASSIGNMENT: Read Chapter 5, "How It Works" and answer homework questions.

• Discuss God concepts, old ideas and new ideas examples.

• Write your old ideas and new ideas about God/Higher Power on a sheet of paper, rip it in half and throw away your old ideas!

BIG BOOK READ: Page 44, Paragraphs 1 through 3

In paragraph one, Bill gives us two questions. (1) If, when you honestly want to, you find you cannot quit entirely (that is the Obsession); and (2) If when drinking, you have little control over the amount you take (that is the Allergy), then you are probably an Alcoholic. We need not ask ourselves anything more than those two questions to determine whether or not we are alcoholics.

Do you see what people do with things? Our Fellowship today has taken those two simple questions and expanded them into a pamphlet that has 44 questions in it. Thank God Ebby didn't have 44 questions when he went into Bill's kitchen. Bill was sitting there drunk, had been drunk for three weeks, and if Ebby had said "Bill, has alcohol been bothering your reputation?" Hell, Bill hadn't had a reputation in years. And if Ebby had said, "Has alcohol been interfering with your sex life?" He hadn't had any of that in years either.

I use the two questions today. If a prospect asks me "Do you think I might be an alcoholic?" I say "I don't know. Let me ask you a question." I ask, "Do you want to quit drinking?" and he says "Yeah." And I ask, "Have you been able to find that you can quit entirely on your own strength?" If he's truly an alcoholic, he's got to say, "No." And I ask, "Do you have little control over the amount you take after you once start drinking?" and a real alcoholic has got to say, "No." And I say "Well, then, you're probably an alcoholic." That's all it takes. There's nothing complicated about it. If the above statements are your case, "you may be suffering from an illness which only a spiritual experience will conquer."

We are the few people in the world who have an <u>illness of the mind and the body</u>, that can only be <u>overcome by a spiritual experience</u>. We realize that we are the only people in the world who have an illness that is a <u>terminal illness,</u> and we can <u>come out of it in better shape</u> than when we went into it.

Paragraph 3 has two words that need to be defined.

<u>Atheist</u>   One who says that God does not exist. If a person really believes that, there is no power on earth for him greater than human power. The only power that he can depend upon is his own mind, he can't really trust other people. Since there is no God, he must run his own show, effect his own destiny and make his own decisions. So, are you an Atheist?

<u>Agnostic</u>   One who believes God exists, but because you cannot prove it to him, he acts as though God does not exist. He runs his own show, effects his own decisions. Stands on his own two feet and rules his own destiny. In other words, he acts exactly as the atheist does, yet he believes that God exists. So, are you an Agnostic?

But for either one, Atheist or Agnostic, we are going to have to find some way to have this Spiritual Experience, and to use this Power greater than human power. For many of us, that seems to be an impossible task. Let's see how we make that transition. "How do I get from that state to the state of being a True Believer?" A true believer is one who believes in God and acts as if he does. He doesn't stand on his own two feet, doesn't run his own show, doesn't rule his own destiny. He turns to God for help and gets the guidance and the strength and the power that he needs, and he knows that God exists. Even the atheist will admit that there's such a thing as evolution and if evolution isn't evidence of some Power greater than human power, I don't know what is. I think most of us are agnostics when we get to AA. We believe in God, but we don't turn to God for help and direction. We run our own show. And we get the same results as the atheist.

BIG BOOK READ: Page 44, Paragraph 4, to Page 45, Paragraph 2

I've never met an alcoholic yet who didn't have a code of morals. I've never met an alcoholic yet who didn't have a philosophy for life. We know what we should do and what we shouldn't do. We know how we should live and how we shouldn't live. But our problem is because of our alcoholism we are unable to live up to those codes, those philosophies, and those morals.

It does not say "which will **help you** solve your problem." It says, "which will solve your problem." Interestingly enough, from this point on we are through talking about alcohol. From Page 45 on, we will talk about one thing and one thing only: How we can find this Power. If we can find the Power, then the Power will solve the problem. And we know for every one of us the main problem is a lack of power. If you and I had the power to solve our problem, we would not have become members of Alcoholics Anonymous. We were driven here under the lash of alcoholism. We came here because we are powerless over alcohol. If we're powerless, we lack the power, and the obvious answer is power, and the question is, whether you are atheist or agnostic, how do you find the Power? Surely, we're not true believers because if we were, we would have had the Power before we came to AA. We can get this Power and apply it in our lives in order to overcome our disease. Now if we're atheist or agnostic, maybe we can change to a true believer and find that Power, and then that Power will solve our problem. The rest of the chapter is devoted to how do you find that Power. The whole rest of the Book is devoted to that one subject.

BIG BOOK READ: Page 45, Paragraph 3, to Page 47, Paragraph 2

He says upon this simple cornerstone a wonderful effective spiritual structure can be built. Believing, that is all we have to do to get started with this program, to believe or to become willing. This is the beginning. Bill said that this is the cornerstone. Remember when we took Step One? Step One is the willingness to change. Once you see that you're powerless over alcohol and your life has become unmanageable and that this isn't going to work, then you become willing to change. That's the foundation. And once the foundation is laid, on that foundation we can lay a cornerstone. After you become willing to change, then you must believe you can change. Step Two is the cornerstone.

Notice the asterisk at the bottom of the page. Please be sure to read Appendix II on "Spiritual Experience." This is the third time we have been referred to read the Spiritual Experience. The wonderfully effective spiritual structure is this vital spiritual experience. We are going to see as we progress through the Steps, we are building that spiritual experience, or that spiritual structure. We have already put two of the stones in place. We are already building the structure as we are going through the Book chapter by chapter.

BIG BOOK READ: Page 47, Paragraph 3, to Page 48, Paragraph 1

All you must do to start out here is to believe. Believing comes before you do something, and faith comes after you believe and then act. Today, how can you not believe that there must be some Power working within this Fellowship of Alcoholics Anonymous? When you first come in here, you don't know that to be true, but you can believe it. And if you stay with us long enough and work the program and have a spiritual experience, then you'll know. And that is faith. But "Faith without works is dead."

BIG BOOK READ: Page 48, Paragraph 3, to Page 51, Paragraph 1

The reason we've got everything we've got today and that's been developed within the last century is not because of man's intellect. Students of ancient history tell us that the intellect of men in ancient days was equal to the best today. I used to think we invented this stuff because we were smarter. But we really aren't. People who lived thousands of years ago were just as smart as we are today. "Yet in ancient times material progress was painfully slow." Very little of this stuff was developed years ago.

Thousands of years ago, 500 years ago, you were not allowed to believe differently. You couldn't believe anything different because of superstition. Tradition and fixed ideas kept you from believing differently and you couldn't change anything. It's only in the last 100 years that our minds have been freed in the realm of the material to believe differently. The reason we went to the moon is because somebody believed we could do that. Same reason we have microwaves, cars, television.

Columbus did show a lot of mannerisms of an alcoholic. The first one was when he left, he didn't know where he was going. That's a drunk. The second, when he got there, he didn't know where he was. And third, when he got back, he didn't know where he had been. But what really made him an alcoholic was a woman financed the whole trip. They say he did die in jail as well.

Columbus did not know but he said, "I believe that the world is round." And he acted on that simple belief—he didn't have any faith. He knew when he came back. But before he left, he just believed. Believe and take action and you will acquire faith.

We would like to sit here and tell you today that the Twelve Steps of Alcoholics Anonymous are brand new and that the world has never seen anything like them. But if we did, we'd tell you a lie because they're based on the same formula Columbus used. Step One. You become willing. Circumstances make you willing to do something about it. Step Two. You come to believe. Step Three. You make a decision. Steps Four through Nine. You take action. And at the end of Step Nine, you get the Promises which are the results of the actions taken in Steps Four through Nine. And in Step Twelve, having had a spiritual awakening, you will then know. Then those of us that know can go back and help the next person become willing to believe, providing they are willing. We cannot make them willing, but we can help them believe if they are willing—if they've drunk enough alcohol, if they've hurt enough and are willing to change, then we can help them believe that they can change. And that's all there is to this program. I thought this would be so complicated that I would never be able to do it. All I have to do is have belief, then decide, and then take action, then I will get results and then I'll have faith. This little formula has been proven to humankind over and over for thousands of years. But I didn't know that until I read the Big Book of Alcoholics Anonymous.

BIG BOOK READ: *Page 51, Paragraph 2, to Page 55, Top of Page*

Again, we see another illustration of the power of believing and how this power is used. There are other illustrations throughout the Book. Bill talks about electricity. Electricity is a power greater than ourselves. We can harness it, we know how to generate electricity, but we don't know that much about it. They say it's a force of undetermined origin. We don't really know where electricity comes from or where it begins. I think this is like the power we receive from God. Most great powers and all the powers in our universe, we don't know where they come from and we don't have to know about them to use them. Bill talks about the Wright Brothers. How can a bicycle mechanic believe he can build an airplane? But they did believe. The Wright Brothers went out and they believed, and they made a decision, and they took the action by taking the plane out and a lot of times they crashed, but they did not stop. If you fail, it is really simple, all you have to do is change what you believe. Make your decision to change and you'll finally get it right. And that's what they did and finally, they got the plane to fly.

We are the only ones that can allow limitations in our lives. Whatever we believe, we become. So be careful if you believe some bad stuff, you had better watch it because it's going to be a part of your life. If we want to change bad beliefs to good beliefs, we will have to change our minds and begin to believe differently. This sounds like what we read in the "Spiritual Experience" on Page 567.

I think this little story about the Wright Brothers was put in here to show us, since most of us were Agnostics, since most of us believed in God but couldn't prove it, that we are to take a chance. That little story shows us proof is not always right anyhow. I found in my life, that any power greater than human power you really can't prove it one way or another. Only the results of our actions will prove it. God is The same way. I do not have to understand God, and you don't have to prove it to me, for me to be able to use that Power. Now, if I know I need the Power, I know the beginning is the belief. And if I know the formula to find it, about the only thing I have to know is where that Power is, and my Book is complete, it gives me everything I have to have on Page 55, it tells me where to find that Power.

BIG BOOK READ: *Page 55, Paragraph 1, to Page 57, to End of Chapter 4*

I think my Book is telling me that the Power of God dwells within me. I think today that every man, woman, and child on the face of the earth has some form of knowledge inside themselves, and that form of knowledge seems to be able to tell us what we should do and what we should not do, it seems to be able to tell us the difference between right and wrong, it seems to be able to tell us how we should live and how we should not live.

Most of us in our chase for money, power, prestige, and sex, have disregarded that knowledge. We pushed it aside and obscured it. Then we began to operate on a conscious knowledge of the mind, to satisfy our wants, needs, and desires. I think some people want to call that knowledge "common sense." Others call it conscience, and some want to call it the soul. I do not care what we call it, as long as we recognize it's there. Sometimes I've been getting ready to do something and some voice from somewhere would say to me: "I don't think you ought to do that" and I wouldn't pay any attention to it. I'd go right ahead and do it. And I'd get into trouble. Then the same voice would say, "See, I told you not to do that." It's been a part of me all my life.

Now if that's true, and I believe it is, remember in Appendix II we talked about tapping into an unsuspected inner resource of strength that we might want to identify with a Power greater than ourselves or God as we understand Him. If God dwells within me, then He dwells within you. It also means we can have a personal God. I don't have to worry anymore whether it's hellfire or brimstone. If He dwells within me, then He's my own personal God. This has given me a completely new concept of God as I understand Him. It has given me a simple little procedure that, if I will follow it, I will be able to find that Power, and I don't have to know anything, all I have to do is <u>believe, decide, act, and then I'll get results</u>. Then I can go back and help the next person come to believe. I don't believe we could make the decision that we're going to be called upon to make in just a little while without this Chapter. Most spiritual things you read will try to prove God to you. This chapter doesn't do that. It gives you a procedure that, if you will follow it, will prove itself by the results that you receive.

ASSIGNMENT:

In your notebook write what you can believe about a Power greater than yourself. (Examples below) On another page write what you cannot believe about God. As you go forward from this point it will be those things that you believe, or that fit into your conceptions of God, or your higher power, that you will be using. You can be comforted in knowing that "Our own conception, however inadequate, was sufficient to make the approach and to effect a contact with Him." (Page 46.) Read the materials in Chapter 5, Pages 58 to 63 (*i.e.,* through the part which concludes with Step Three). Also answer the assignment questions.

GOD CONCEPT EXAMPLES:

Old Ideas/Prejudices about God	**New Ideas About God**
Went to church a lot	Loving, kind, personal God
Went to a lot of different churches	God doesn't judge me
Went to church just on holidays	God created me
Going to Hell	God gives me power, peace, happiness,
Judgmental God	and a sense of direction
	God lives and resides in my heart

Write your old ideas and new ideas about God/Higher Power on a sheet of paper, rip it in half and throw away your old ideas!

ASSIGNMENT: Read Chapter 5, "How It Works", Answer homework questions for "How It Works".

HOW IT WORKS QUESTIONS

PAGE 60

1.   Do you question whether you are capable of being honest with yourself? (If you do—you're not.)

NOTE: The state of mind you are asked to be in when you start the Steps is honesty, fearlessness, thoroughness, and a willingness to go to any length.

2.   What do half measures avail us?

3.   Are you convinced that a life run on self-will can hardly be a success?

4.   Can you see the effects of self-centeredness in your life?

5.   Have you been self-centered?

LIST: Examples of your self-centeredness in your notebook.

PAGE 62

6.   Did you know that you could not reduce self-centeredness much by wishing or trying on your own power?

7.   Are you willing to make the decisions set forth at the bottom of Page 62?

PAGE 63

8.   Are you willing to take this Step?

NOTE: The Third Step Promises that follow the taking of Step Three are described in the paragraph at the top of Page 63.

WEEK 7 - HOW IT WORKS, PART 1
(Step Three)

Instructions - How It Works, Part 1

• BIG BOOK Read - Page 58, Paragraph 1 to (a) (b) (c) on Page 60
• Workbook Read, including a portion of Chapter Five from the original manuscript
• BIG BOOK Read - Page 60, Paragraph 3 to Page 62, Paragraph 2
• Workbook Read
• BIG BOOK Read - Page 62, Paragraph 3
• Workbook Read
• Discuss the "Keystone Chart"
• BIG BOOK Read - Page 63, Paragraphs 1 to 3
• Workbook Read
• Discuss the "Road Chart to Decision"

It was suggested to us when we started this workshop to have the group recite the Third Step Prayer (Page 63, Paragraph 3), on their knees together.

ASSIGNMENT: Continue reading Page 63, Paragraph 4 through the end of the Chapter. You should be prepared to start your Fourth Step next week. Continue to say the Third Step Prayer every morning in your mediation time.

BIG BOOK READ: Page 58, Paragraph 1 to (a) (b) (c) on Page 60

Now we have completed the Chapter, "To The Agnostics." We have laid the foundation and have established the first two Steps.

Keep in mind the problems that Bill was having with the first forty people. Writing the Book was quite a task. Bill was writing the Book in Hank's office in New Jersey and his secretary, Ruth Hock, would type these chapters out as Bill stood behind her. As these chapters were finished, they were sent to the Akron and New York groups. The groups would go over each chapter and every word. This was a real task, we really don't know what they went through to get this Book written. Ruth said, "I had to type this manuscript 44 times before it was finally printed."

Bill had completed the first four chapters and felt the groundwork had been laid. He felt it was now time for the <u>main purpose of the Book,</u> to <u>show alcoholics how to recover.</u> Prior to writing this chapter he was having trouble, he prayed for guidance and then laid down. After a few minutes, he picked up his pad and pencil and began to write. He said that it seemed as though his

59

pencil had a mind of its own. In thirty minutes, he had written "How It Works" and the Twelve Steps. He really didn't know how many steps he needed as he started. He had the six steps from the Oxford Group. He knew the steps needed expanding to close the loopholes that drunks would jump through. When he finished, he numbered them and noticed there were Twelve Steps and equated this with the twelve apostles.

He had just finished the Steps when Howard, a New York member, stopped by to see him. Howard had a newcomer with him. They looked at the Steps and neither one of them liked them. Both started giving Bill hell about the Steps. You know how alcoholics are—they don't like change. They had six steps in the Oxford Group and didn't care for him doubling the Steps. How would you feel if you went to a meeting and suddenly you had 24 Steps? There were a lot of discussions and arguments in the groups. This was probably only one of the crises in writing the Big Book. The writing of the Book stopped, and they went through a great dilemma. Some changes were made, and they were able to go on with the Book.

Now we are going to read what Bill wrote that night as it appears in the Original Manuscript.

"FROM THE ORIGINAL MANUSCRIPT"
(You can purchase this from the AA Central Office)

CHAPTER FIVE

HOW IT WORKS

Rarely have we seen a person fail who has thoroughly followed our <u>directions</u>. Those who do not recover are people who cannot or will not completely give themselves to this simple program, usually men and women who are constitutionally incapable of being honest with themselves. There are such unfortunates. They are not at fault; they seem to have been born that way. They are naturally incapable of grasping and developing <u>a way of life</u> that demands rigorous honesty. Their chances are less than average. There are those, too, who suffer from grave emotional and mental disorders, but many of them do recover if they have the capacity to be honest.

Our stories disclose in a general way what we used to be like, what happened, and what we are like now. If you have decided you want what we have and are willing to go to any length to get it—then you are ready to <u>follow directions</u>.

At some of these, <u>you may balk</u>. <u>You</u> may think you can find an easier, softer way. <u>We doubt if you can</u>. With all the earnestness at our command, we beg of you to be fearless and thorough from the very start. Some of us have tried to hold on to our old ideas and the result was nil until we let go absolutely.

Remember that <u>you</u> are dealing with alcohol—cunning, baffling, powerful! Without help, it is too much for <u>you</u>. But there is one who has all power—that one is God. <u>You must find Him now!</u>

Half measures will <u>avail you nothing</u>. <u>You</u> stand at the turning point. <u>Throw yourself under His protection and care with complete abandon.</u>

<u>Now we think you can take it!</u> Here are the steps we took, which are suggested as <u>your</u> program of recovery:

1. Admitted we were powerless over alcohol—that our lives had become   unmanageable.

2. Came to believe that a power greater than ourselves could restore us to sanity.

3. Made a decision to turn our will and our lives over to the care and <u>direction</u> of God as we understood Him.

4. Made a searching and fearless moral inventory of ourselves.

5. Admitted to God, to ourselves, and to another human being the exact nature of our wrongs.

6. Were entirely <u>willing that God</u> remove all these defects of character.

7. Humbly, <u>on our knees</u>, asked Him to remove our shortcomings—<u>holding nothing back</u>.

8. Made a list of all persons we had harmed and became willing to make <u>complete</u> amends to them all.

9. Made direct amends to such people wherever possible, except when to do so would injure them or others.

10. Continued to take personal inventory and when we were wrong promptly admitted it.

11. Sought through prayer and meditation to improve our contact with God, praying only for knowledge of His will for us and the power to carry that out.

12. Having had a spiritual <u>experience</u> as a result of this <u>course of action</u>, we tried to carry this message to <u>others, especially alcoholics</u>, and to practice these principles in all our affairs.

<u>You</u> may exclaim, "What an order. I can't go through with it." Do not be discouraged. No one among us has been able to maintain anything like perfect adherence to these principles. We are not saints. The point is that we are willing to grow along spiritual lines. The principles we have set down are guides to progress. We claim spiritual progress rather than spiritual perfection.

Our description of the alcoholic, the chapter to the agnostic, and our personal adventures before and after, have been <u>designed to sell you</u> three pertinent ideas:

(a)   That you are alcoholic and cannot manage your own life.

(b)   That probably no human power can relieve your alcoholism.

(c)   That God <u>can and will</u>.

<u>If you are not convinced on these vital issues, you ought to re-read the book to this point or else throw it away!</u>

============== * * * ==============

We think with that final statement, Bill makes it clear what he has been trying to convey to us. He has been using the Doctor's Opinion and the first four chapters to sell us three pertinent ideas. Those three pertinent ideas are contained in Step One and Step Two. If you are not convinced, you should read the book again or throw it away.

The very next thing he is going to start us on is Step Three. If you don't have Step One and Step Two you can't do Step Three. Before the Book was written, they would go out to the hospital, jails, or wherever, and by sharing their story, they would convince their man that he was an alcoholic also. Through talking about the disease, the physical allergy, and the obsession of the mind, they could help him see his problem and take Step One.

Then they would ask if they could come back in a day or two. They would come back and begin talking about spirituality, telling him how they had found it necessary to find a <u>Power greater than human power</u>, and how they apply it in their lives in order to recover. They would help this alcoholic that had already identified with them, to be able to take what we know today as Step Two.

Then they would take him to an Oxford Group meeting. They would present him to the meeting, telling the meeting that they have been talking with him, and they were convinced that he knows he is an alcoholic. We are also convinced that he believes that God can restore him to sanity, and we want to sponsor him into the group. That is what sponsorship was in the beginning.

Then the group would vote on whether or not to take him into the group. After he was voted into the group, two or three of them would take him upstairs in Dr. Bob's house. They would get down on their knees and he would make his surrender, which we know today as Step Three.

If you are sold on Steps One and Two, you are now ready to take Step Three. From Step Three on, the Big Book tells us with every Step, <u>why you need to take it, how to take it, and what the results will be</u>. It does not do that with Steps One and Two. They are not <u>working steps</u>. Steps One and Two are <u>conclusions of the mind</u> that we draw based upon the information presented to us in the Doctor's Opinion and the first four chapters.

I think it is also clear that Bill meant for these Steps to be a <u>set of individual directions</u>, for the <u>individuals to recover</u>. Because he kept saying <u>you</u>. He did not call them <u>suggestions</u>, he called them <u>directions</u>.

Immediately when the rest of the Fellowship saw this, that's when they got upset. Changing from six steps to twelve steps was bad enough, but what they didn't like was the word "directions." They said, "Bill, you can't give an alcoholic <u>direction</u>. If you try, he won't do a damned thing." Another bunch said it wasn't hard enough and they argued back and forth. They said, instead of saying <u>you</u>, we should say <u>we</u> had to. Bill didn't want to change it and the group said he would, because it was their book, not his.

Finally, Bill realized that he was going to have to accommodate some of their wishes. With the suggestions of a non-alcoholic psychiatrist, they made a few changes. He said if you drop directions and make it suggestions, if you quit saying <u>you</u> and say <u>we</u>, quit saying <u>must</u> and use <u>ought</u>, probably people would use the Book a little more. As a <u>compromise</u> between the fundamental <u>Christians and the Atheists</u>, they decided on <u>God, as we understand Him</u>. With those thoughts in mind, they changed "How It Works" to what we have in our Book today.

Now, Bill is a real alcoholic—cunning, baffling, and powerful. He said, "Okay, I'll agree to your changes. But I'm going to make a deal with you right here. I'm tired of fighting over this Book. I'm not going to fight with you anymore. If I am to finish the Book, you'll have to let me be the final authority, from here on out." They didn't want to do that at all, but they didn't want to write it either. They agreed to let Bill be the final authority from here on.

What he knew that they didn't, was that he was going to put <u>directions</u> back in the Book, two pages later. The rest of the way through the Book he's going to put <u>you</u> and <u>must</u> also. This is the story of "How It Works" as it is written today.

BIG BOOK READ: Page 60, Paragraph 3 to Page 62, Paragraph 2

There are three words in Step Three that need to be defined. If we can understand them as the writer understood them, then it makes Step Three easy.

> <u>**Decision**</u>: The word "decision" implies there are going to be further <u>actions taken</u>.

Note: One of the problems many of us have in Step Three is that we think if we take Step Three, we will turn our will and our lives over to the care of God as we understand Him. But the Step says we <u>make a decision</u> to do that. If <u>we could turn it over in Step Three</u>, we wouldn't need the rest of the Steps. If we make a decision to do something, we are going to take a certain action. <u>The action that we need to take is in Steps Four through Nine.</u>

<u>All my actions are born in my thought</u>! If the <u>thinking is right</u> then the <u>actions are right</u>, and usually the <u>life is okay</u>. If the <u>thinking is lousy</u>, the <u>actions are lousy,</u> and the <u>life goes to hell in a handbasket</u>.

Will: Our will is nothing more than <u>our mind</u>. The power of <u>choosing what to do</u> and our <u>thinking</u>.

Life: My life is nothing more than <u>my actions</u>. What I am today is the <u>sum of all the actions</u> I have <u>taken in the past</u>.

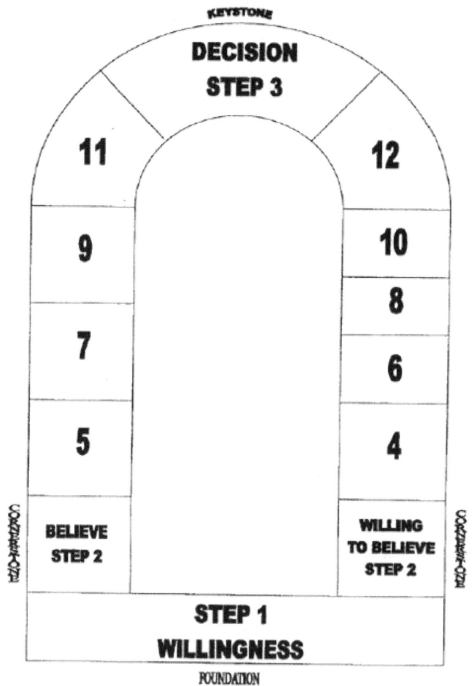

ROAD CHART TO DECISION

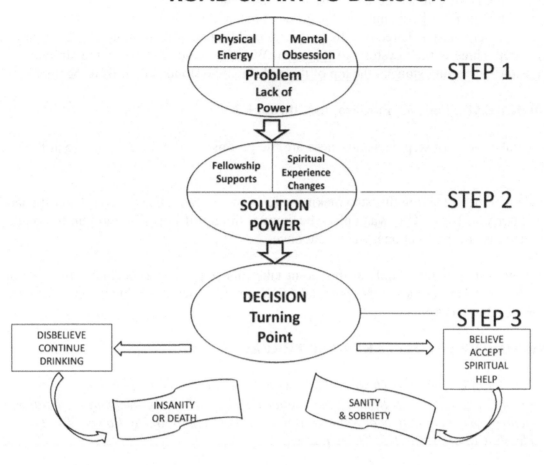

BIG BOOK READ: Page 62, Paragraph 3

"This concept was the keystone of the new and triumphant arch through which we passed to freedom." Again, we can see he is adding to the structure. In Step One, <u>willingness was the foundation</u>. In Step Two, <u>believing was the cornerstone</u>, and we didn't even know what we were building. Now here in Step Three he tells us we are building an arch through which we passed to freedom. Step Three is the <u>keystone in this arch</u>. We gain another stone in the structure. The <u>keystone</u> is the supporting <u>stone at the top of the arch;</u> it is the stone that holds it together.

BIG BOOK READ: Page 63, Paragraphs 1 through 3

When we make the third step decision, these are the promises we will receive here at the top of page 63.

We thought well before taking this step making sure we were ready; that we could at last abandon ourselves utterly to Him. This was only a beginning, though if honestly and humbly made, an effect, sometimes a very great one, was felt at once.

When in a workshop many people at this point take this step with an understanding person or spiritual advisor. Many groups at this point take this Step together and recite the prayer that is set forth on Page 63 at this time.

WE ARE NOW READY TO TAKE STEP THREE:

> *"God, I offer myself to Thee—to build with me and to do with me as Thou wilt. Relieve me of the bondage of self, that I may better do Thy will. Take away my difficulties, that victory over them may bear witness to those I would help of Thy Power, Thy Love, and Thy Way of life. May I do Thy will always*!"

You should be prepared to start your Fourth Step next week. *Continue to* say the Third Step Prayer in morning meditation

ASSIGNMENT: Continue reading Page 63, Paragraph 4 through the end of the chapter.

We will be working with Columns 1 and 2 of the Review of Resentments Form.

Instructions – How It Works, Part 2

• BIG BOOK Read - Page 63, Paragraph 4 to Page 64, Top of Page
• Workbook Read
• BIG BOOK Read - Page 64, Paragraphs 1 and 2
• Workbook Read
• Discuss Bill's Business Inventory
• BIG BOOK Read - Page 64, Paragraph 3 to Page 65, Top of Page
• Workbook Read
• Discuss the Grudge List Form and the Resentment/Grudge List Examples
• BIG BOOK Read - Page 65, Paragraph 1 to Page 66, Paragraph 2
• Workbook Read
• Discuss Columns 1 and 2 (Review of Resentment Form)

ASSIGNMENT: Complete Grudge List and Columns 1 and 2; refer to Bill's Business Inventory; read Page 66, Paragraph 3, to Page 67, Paragraph 1 (preparing for Column 3).

BIG BOOK READ: Page 63, Paragraph 4 to Page 64, Top of Page

Always there has been <u>God's will</u> and always there has been <u>my will</u>. I could have been operating on God's will all the time but there seems to have been something within my will, within my mind, that blocked me off from God's will.

If I am going to turn my will and my life over to the care of God as I understand Him, I am first going to have to find out what is within me that is <u>blocking me off from God's will</u> – and do something about its elimination before God can begin to direct my thinking. Then we can open up space in our heads for God's will to come into our minds.

A time element is involved in this paragraph; it says that we take this Step <u>at once</u>. We heard a professional counselor not long ago, telling people to wait two or three years to take their inventory. Our question to him is, how many people have you killed with that statement?

We are trying to find a way to have peace of mind, serenity, and happiness. As long as we are running our lives on self-will, we cannot have that. We didn't have it before we got here on self-will, and we won't have it after we get here on self-will. The longer we put off taking Step Four the greater the chance of us getting drunk.

We think one of the reasons we procrastinate and put it off is <u>fear</u>. Fear that we dare not look at this stuff and we sure don't want to show it to someone else. Fear that we can't do it <u>perfectly</u> and would rather wait until we can do it right. If that is our reason for not taking Step Four, what we are really saying is, let's get well and then we'll do it. But we need to do Step Four in order to get well.

Another reason we put it off is, we really don't know how to do it and we have a lot of confusion in taking Step Four. Somewhere down the line, somebody was looking at Step Five and there was a statement that said something about all your life story. We took a statement out of Step Five and began to write our life story as our inventory for Step Four. I did that when I first tried to take this inventory.

I didn't learn a thing because everything I wrote down, I already knew. I learned nothing new by writing my life story. As I look back at it, I realize that 95% of it doesn't have anything to do with my drinking anyway. The 95% of my story obscured the 5% that did have something to do with it.

BIG BOOK READ: Page 64, Paragraphs 1 and 2; then refer to Bill's Business Inventory

Bill is going to tell us how to take a business inventory assuming that we know something about business. And then after he tells us how to take a business inventory, he's going to turn right around and say we do the same thing with our lives. In other words, we're going to take a personal inventory just like he tells us to take this business inventory. Therefore, we started upon a personal inventory. This was Step Four. And immediately he jumps to a business. He says a business that takes no regular inventory usually goes broke. I think one of his first valid comparisons between the business inventory and the personal inventory is this:

In our personal lives, you and I have a business which to us is the most important business in the world. And that's the business of finding a way to live where we can be sober and peaceful and happy and free and not have to go back to drinking. And if we do not inventory ourselves once in a while, then we may end up going broke, which is going back and getting drunk all over again. So, the first comparison between the two would be that we, without taking the inventory, would probably go broke or get drunk, just like a business goes broke.

Now Bill says, taking a commercial inventory/business inventory is a fact-finding and a fact-facing process. Step Four inventory comparison:

On the right side, we put <u>PERSONAL</u> and on the left side, we put <u>BUSINESS</u>. A commercial inventory is <u>1)</u> a fact-finding and <u>2)</u> a fact-facing process. It is <u>3)</u> an effort to discover the truth about <u>4)</u> the stock in trade. One object is to disclose <u>5)</u> damaged or unsalable goods; <u>6)</u> to get rid of them promptly and without regret. It's the only way the business is to be successful. A businessman cannot fool himself about values. We have taken some key words and put them on the left side under <u>BUSINESS</u>: fact-finding, fact-facing, truth about the stock in trade, your effort to disclose damaged or unsalable goods, to get rid of them promptly and without regret.

Now Bill says, we did exactly the same thing with our lives. We did with our lives what he just told us to do with the business inventory. Now this guy loves words, and he loves words that mean the same thing. Let's look at our Step Four:

We made a <u>1)</u> searching (and we put this straight across from fact-finding; they basically mean the same thing); and a <u>2)</u> fearless (and we put this word across from fact-facing); and <u>3)</u> moral. And we saw the word "moral," and thought, there's that list of dirty, filthy, nasty items and we don't want to look at them and we don't want anybody else to see them, so we dare not take this inventory.

I went to the dictionary again and looked up the word "<u>moral</u>." It does not mean a list of dirty, filthy, nasty items. If Bill had wanted us to make a list of those things, he probably would have said to make a searching and fearless "amoral" or "immoral" inventory. He didn't say that, he said "moral." "Moral," according to the dictionary, is "<u>the truth about the facts</u>." That's all it is— <u>the truth about something</u>, the difference between the <u>right and wrong</u> of a situation.

We make a <u>searching and fearless "truthful" inventory of ourselves</u>. Now we are the only stock-in-trade that we have in our business of staying sober. Now what part of us determines whether we're going to stay sober or not? Is it our bodies? No. It's our thinking apparatus. If we make this searching and fearless moral inventory of ourselves, our stock-in-trade, we're going to inventory our "thinking." One object of this is to <u>4)</u> disclose damage and unsalable thinking and <u>5)</u> to get rid of it promptly and without regret, because that is the very thing that <u>blocks us off from God's will</u>. If my thinking is okay, God can probably direct my will and I'll be successful in the business of staying sober. If my thinking is lousy, then God cannot direct my will and I will probably be unsuccessful and end up broke and getting drunk. I'm going to do the same thing in Step Four that he just told me to do with the business inventory.

BILL'S BUSINESS INVENTORY COMPARED TO A PERSONAL INVENTORY

BUSINESS INVENTORY	PERSONAL INVENTORY
FACT-FINDING	SEARCHING
FACT-FACING	FEARLESS
TRUTH	MORAL
STOCK IN TRADE	OURSELVES
DAMAGED, UNSALABLE GOODS	OLD THOUGHT PROCESSES
Businessman cannot fool himself about the value of his products!	**We must get rid of old thought patterns without regret!**

We have learned that we have a three-fold disease: we are physically, mentally, and spiritually sick. For physical illness, we go to the doctor. Whatever that illness may be, it will display certain symptoms. The doctor will read those symptoms, diagnose and prescribe for me and hopefully, I will get well.

If I am mentally ill, I will go to a psychiatrist. My mental illness will display certain symptoms. The psychiatrist will diagnose and prescribe for me and hopefully, I will get well.

If I am spiritually ill, I will also display certain symptoms. The manifestations or symptoms of spiritual illness are: Resentment, "madder than hell all the time." Fear, "scared to death all the time." Guilt and Remorse, associated with Harms or Hurts done during our drinking careers.

If I want to get rid of what blocks me off from God, I will have to get rid of resentment, fear, guilt, and remorse.

That is the process we are now beginning. If those things can leave my head, then God's will can come in. This is the prescription in the Book and hopefully, I will get well.

FOURTH STEP INVENTORY PROCESS

RESENTMENTS-THE NUMBER ONE OFFENDER (COLUMNS 1 AND 2)

From these thoughts or mental attitudes "stem all forms of spiritual disease." We are instructed to list all people, institutions, or principles with whom we were angry or had resentments toward. What is a resentment?

A. Webster's Dictionary defines "Resentment" as "Indignation" or ill-will felt as a result of a real or imagined offense. Then Webster's refers the reader to the word "Anger" and gives other examples of this thought or feeling, which include rage, fury, ire, wrath, resentment, and indignation. These words denote varying degrees of displeasure from anger—strong, intense, and explosive—to the longer-lasting resentment—ill-will and suppressed anger generated by a sense of being wronged or being wrong.

B. In summary and broadly defined, we are dealing with a negative or unpleasant thought or feeling caused or generated by a real or imagined act or failure to act of a person, institution or principle.

C. Persons, institutions, or principles may need some explanation. Remember you are a "person" and your action or failure to act may very well cause you to think or feel badly (generally, this is called "guilt"). Institutions are any group of people, authorities, companies, governmental agencies, or other organizations.

A principle is a basic truth or law. Many of these basic truths or laws have and do offend us, for example:

1. Alcoholism is an incurable, progressive disease.
2. Honesty is the best policy.
3. As you give, you receive (each of us suffers the consequences of his own action, there is no free lunch).
4. When you are disturbed, no matter what the cause, there is something wrong with you.
5. A life lived without self-examination is not worth living. (Socrates)

PREPARING THE GRUDGE LIST

With the foregoing instructions in mind and before proceeding any further with this inventory, a list should be prepared. On the next page, there is a separate piece of paper set up for your Grudge List. As defined above, put down the names of people, institutions, or principles which have caused you to have a resentment. Certain points should be remembered.

(1) If you can remember the resentment, you should list it, even though you think you are "Over It." Go back through your life. "Nothing counts but thoroughness and honesty."

(2) Some people start recalling the earliest memories and work forward. I personally like to do it the way Bill did. <u>Pray, be still, and let God put the thoughts in my mind He wants me to work on at this time</u>. Because, as we stay sober, more will be revealed. We can take this same action in Step Ten later.

(3) Throughout the taking of Step Five and at times thereafter, you will recall other people, institutions, and principles which have caused these negative thoughts and feelings. You can add to this list at any time, but do not spend too much time worrying about how complete the list is, simply do the best you can.

(4) Do not concern yourself with whether you should or should not have the feelings, just make the list and nothing more at this point.

(5) When the Grudge List is complete, transfer everything on the Grudge List to Column 1.

YOUR GRUDGE LIST

PEOPLE	INSTITUTIONS	PRINCIPLES

GRUDGE LIST EXAMPLES

Here is a list of people, institutions, and principles that may be helpful in your resentment inventory. Feel free to add to the list if you need to.

People	Institutions	Principles
Father (step)	Marriage	God-deity
Mother (step)	Bible	Retribution
Sister (step)	Church	Ten Commandments
Brother (step)	Religion	Jesus Christ
Aunts	Races	Satan
Uncles	Law	Death
Cousins	Authority	Life after death
Clergy	Government	Heaven
Police	Educational system	Hell
Lawyers	Correctional system	Sin
Judges	Mental health system	Adultery
Doctors	Philosophy	Golden rule
Employers	Nationality	Original sin
Employees		Seven deadly sins
Co-workers		
In-Laws		
Husbands		
Wives		
Creditors		
Childhood friends		
School friends		
Teachers		
Lifelong friends		
Best friends		
Acquaintances		
Girlfriends		
Boyfriends		
Parole officers		
Probation officers		
Program friends		
Military friends		

REVIEW OF RESENTMENTS

Column 1	Column 2	Column 3									Page
I am resentful at	The cause	Which part of self is affected									67
		Social			Security			Sex			¶ 1
We listed people, institutions, or principles with which we were angry.	We asked ourselves why we were angry.	Self-Esteem	Relationship	Ambition	Material	Emotional	Ambition	Acceptable	Hidden	Ambition	Prayer

BIG BOOK READ: Page 65, Paragraph 1 to Page 66, Paragraph 2

Listing Our Resentments (Column 2)

Now we come to the <u>Review of Resentments form</u>. After we listed the people in Column 1, we come to the second column and look at the cause, what did they do? And we put the answer beside each resentment. Again, we go from top to bottom. What was the cause of that resentment? We all remember that. If we didn't know this, we wouldn't remember the name. We all have that information. There may be one cause by one name and several causes by another name. The following procedure has proven helpful in this understanding and analysis:

1.   Take the first name from your "Grudge List" and write it in Column 1 on the first page.

2.   In Column 2, write a few words which describe every event or circumstance you can recall which causes you to resent the person named in Column 1. This is a very important part of the analysis. We learn from specific events, not general complaints. We learn little from the complaint that "He was always lying." But we learn much from a specific "He told me he wasn't married."

For instance, in Bill's, he is resentful at Mr. Brown and the cause is his attention to my wife; told my wife of my mistress; and Brown may get my job at the office. I'd get a little upset with Brown, too. He's mad at Mrs. Jones: She's a nut, she snubbed me; she committed her husband for drinking and he's my friend; she's a gossip. He's mad at his employer: he's unreasonable, unjust, overbearing (he probably said, "Bill, where the hell were you on Monday?"), he also threatens to fire me for drinking and for padding my expense account (now that's unreasonable). He is mad at his wife: She misunderstands and nags; she likes old Brown; and she wants the house put in her name. Now you tie together liking Brown and wanting the house in her name and it's about time to get a little upset here.

Very carefully beside each name, from top to bottom, we list the cause. I've never seen an alcoholic yet who does not only know who they are mad at, but we know exactly why and what we're mad at. All we've got to do is take it out of our heads and put it down on a piece of paper. When we finish column 2, I think we're going to realize something. It's not really those people we're upset with, it's what they did to us that got us upset. So, the first thing we realize is that it is not so much the people we are upset with, it's what they've done to us that got us upset. Very valuable. We're going to need that after a while.

ASSIGNMENT: Complete Columns 1 and 2 of the Review of Resentments form; Read Page 66, Paragraph 3, to Page 67, Paragraph 1 about Column 3. Complete Grudge List

We will be working with Column 3 of the Review of Resentments form.

Instructions - How It Works, Part 3

• BIG BOOK Read - Page 64, Paragraph 3 to Page 66, Paragraph 2 (repeat from last week)
• Workbook Read
• BIG BOOK Read - Page 66, Paragraph 3 to Page 67, Paragraph 1
• Workbook Read
• Discuss "The Basic Instincts of Life Chart"
• Workbook Read
• Discuss Column 3 Instructions

ASSIGNMENT: Complete Column 3 and read Page 67, Paragraph 2 (preparing for Column 4).

BIG BOOK READ: Page 64, Paragraph 3 to Page 66, Paragraph 2 (Repeat from Last Week)

Now you see why you had to have a <u>written inventory</u>. If you only had a <u>mental inventory</u>, you would have already lost it. But now, we can turn back to this list and look at it again, for it holds the key to the future. We've been looking at the past according to resentments, but the past resentments are going to hold the key for the future if we can see what to do with them.

Always before, I looked at my resentments to see what those people had done to me. Today I'm looking at it to see what those resentments did to me. And if the resentment blocks me off from God's will and causes me to get drunk, then I can't afford to have the resentment. And it doesn't make any difference whether it's justified or unjustified. Either one of them effectively blocks me off from God's will.

BIG BOOK READ: Page 66, Paragraph 3 to Page 67, Paragraph 1

We began to see that the world and its people really dominated us. In that state, the wrongdoings of others, fancied or real, had power to actually kill.

And when I read that statement, I suddenly realized that other people have been telling me what to do all my life through my resentment toward them. When I'm resenting them, they have control of my thinking. And if they control my thinking, they effectively control my decisions and my actions, and my entire life. I always thought I did that but, I realize today that I never did. They've always controlled me. When I saw that I said, "The hell with it." I'm not going to let those people live in my head rent-free anymore. I made a decision in Step Three to let God direct my thinking. Now if other people, dead or alive, direct my thinking, then God can't. I did not know that until I took this inventory. Resentments come from self-will. God makes self-will and only God has the power to overcome self-will. Self cannot overcome self. But the instant I see what those resentments are doing to me, I am just about willing to do anything to get rid of them rather than let them get me drunk.

We put our resentments down, list them, and analyze them. We have three columns and we read them across. We can learn a lot from them. We can analyze them when we get them on paper. We could not analyze them when they were in our minds. This is sort of like a little computer. You have to have the first column down. If the name is down, we can extract the cause. Once we get the cause, we can trace the cause and find out which part of self it affects. Then for the first time, we can get a pretty good picture of the truth of the resentment. Now when we do this, we're getting rid of about 95% of these resentments simply by listing and analyzing them. Most of us alcoholics think of ourselves as intelligent people.

When you list and analyze the resentments, about 95% of them are going to look dumb. They look stupid on paper. And we get rid of them. There will be some that will dig in. With those deep-seated resentments, Bill suggests that we use prayer on those. There is no way that you can enter a relationship with God and the communion with God in prayer about the well-being of another individual and at the same time continue to resent him. One will remove the other. There is no way.

In the program, we tend to focus on the Third and Seventh Step prayers. Hardly anyone ever mentions the FOURTH STEP PRAYER that appears on Page 67, Paragraph 1. If you have a resentment and you are re-playing it over and over again, you are cutting yourself off from God's will working in your life. This is the prayer you should be praying for yourself about the people on your resentment list.

It's so simple you may think it won't work. But if you follow these simple instructions and do what this Book says, I guarantee you can get rid of resentments and God can direct your thinking in that area of your life. But it would do no good to get rid of them if I didn't know how to keep them from coming back. Because the world is full of sick people, and tomorrow they're going to do something to me just as sure as anything. If I'm not careful, I'll resent, and I can't have even one resentment for very long. If I have one resentment, almost immediately I'll have two, three, etc. and I'm a basket case all over again. I've got one more thing to do before I'm through with resentments. We've got to get down to the cause of this thing. We've got to get rid of the real things within ourselves that started the whole thing.

THE BASIC INSTINCTS OF LIFE:

SOCIAL INSTINCT	SECURITY INSTINCT	SEX INSTINCT
SELF-ESTEEM - What we think of ourselves, high or low. **PERSONAL RELATIONSHIPS** - Our relations with other human beings and the world around us. **AMBITIONS** - Our plans to gain acceptance, power, recognition, prestige, etc.	**MATERIAL** - Wanting money, buildings, property, clothing, etc. in order to be secure in the future. **EMOTIONAL** - Based upon our needs for another person or persons. Some tend to dominate; some are overly dependent on others. **AMBITIONS** - Our plans to gain material wealth, or to dominate, or to depend upon others.	**ACCEPTABLE** - Our sex lives as accepted by Society, God's principles, or our own principles. **HIDDEN** - Our sex lives that are contrary to either Society, God's principles, or our own principles. **AMBITION** - Our plans regarding our sex lives, either acceptable or hidden.
Incorrect judgment causing **RESENTMENTS** Definition: Feelings of bitter hurt or indignation which come from rightly or wrongly held feelings of being injured or offended.	Incorrect belief causing **FEAR** Definition: Feelings of anxiety, restlessness, irritability, discontent, uneasiness, apprehension, etc.	Incorrect actions taken cause **HARMS OR HURTS** Definition: Wrong acts which result in pain, hurt feelings, worry, financial loss, etc. for others and self.

FOURTH STEP INVENTORY PROCESS

COLUMN 3 INSTRUCTIONS

In Column 3, the "Affects My" column: Was it our self-esteem, our security, our ambitions, our personal or sex relations, which had been interfered with? When you have completed your causes column opposite each of the events you have listed in Column 2, you will check which part of self is affected in Column 3.

1. We go to the SELF COLUMN, Column 3. We take the Self-Esteem Column and remembering always to **work from top to bottom**, beside each name and each cause, we asked ourselves: Was it a threat to our self-esteem? Did it put us down in the eyes of other people? Did it embarrass us? Did it affect our communication skills and interactions with others? If so, we put a little checkmark there.

2. Then we come back to the PERSONAL RELATIONSHIP COLUMN. Starting at the top and working to the bottom. Is it a threat to our personal relationships?

3. Then we look at the AMBITIONS COLUMN. Everybody has plans regarding their future. That's a part of our make-up. And I'll get just as upset with you if you threaten what I'm trying to get, as I will if you threaten what I've already got. The only way I can be upset is if you threaten one of the two: My basic instincts or my ambitions in those areas. Were my ambitions to have good personal relationships threatened?

4. Then we come back to the SECURITY COLUMN, do MATERIAL INSTINCTS first. Was it a threat to my material life, job, home, cars, etc.?

5. Then we go to our EMOTIONAL SECURITY. Was it a threat to my emotional security? (EXAMPLE: VERBAL ABUSE THREATENS EMOTIONAL SECURITY.)

6. Then we look at the AMBITIONS COLUMN concerning my SECURITY INSTINCTS. Were my ambitions threatened?

7. Then to the SEX COLUMN. Is it a threat to my ACCEPTABLE SEX LIFE with my spouse, friend, or lover?

8. Then to the SEX COLUMN. Is it a threat to my HIDDEN SEX LIFE with my spouse, friend, or lover?

9. Then we look at the AMBITIONS COLUMN concerning my SEXUAL INSTINCTS. Were my sexual ambitions threatened?

As I fill these out, I begin to realize that I am making an awful lot of checkmarks under one particular column. I finish this column and I realize something that's very important for me to know. First, in the first column, I realize it is not how many people I am mad at, but how much they control my thinking. In the third column, I realize it's not really what they did, it's how I reacted to it based upon my own basic instincts of life. Today, for the first time in my life, I realize where my anger comes from. It's my reaction based on my basic instincts of life to what other people are doing to me, or what I think they are doing to me. Either one is just as bad. Now that I know where anger comes from, I might be able to do something about it. But, until I know that, I'll never get a handle on it, and that anger will keep getting me in trouble for the rest of my life. I've learned three valuable things and all I've done is fill out the sheet.

This Was Our Course

"We realized that the people who wronged us were perhaps spiritually sick. Though we did not like their symptoms and the way these disturbed us, they, like ourselves, were sick too."

We then pray the following prayer for each of the resentments on our inventory and make checks in the column when completed:

God help me show _____ the same tolerance, pity, and patience that I would cheerfully grant a sick friend. _____ is a sick person. How can I be helpful to _____? God save me from being angry. Thy will be done.

We are not praying for them. We are praying for change in ourselves, to help us show them the same tolerance, pity, and patience that we would cheerfully grant a sick friend.

DEFINITIONS:

Tolerance	The ability or willingness to accept or respect behaviors, customs, opinions, or beliefs of others without being affected in an adverse way.
Pity	Feeling of profound sympathy aroused by unhappiness or suffering of another. Heartfelt distress and concern induced by contemplation of another's plight, and unhappiness, sometimes tinged with contempt for his or her weaknesses and inferiority.
Patience	The capability or quality with which you can wait calmly and without complaint. Your ability to endure annoyance, hardship, or difficulties without complaining or losing one's composure.

ASSIGNMENT: Complete Column 3 and read Page 67, Paragraph 2 preparing for Column 4.

We will be working with Column 4 (AA's call this column "our part") of the Review of Resentments form (this Review of Resentments form **only** contains Column 4).

Instructions - How It Works, Part 4

- BIG BOOK Read - Page 67, Paragraph 2
- Workbook Read
- Discuss Column 4 Instructions
- Review of Resentments form

ASSIGNMENT: Complete your Column 4.

BIG BOOK READ: Page 67, Paragraph 2

The first symptom of spiritual illness is resentment. We have taken our inventory of resentments. Many of us are holding on to resentments from the past. We are sitting around tables trying to analyze why they did that to us. It doesn't make any difference why they did it, they did it. Then we try and analyze why those resentments made us the way we are today. And it doesn't make any difference, that's the way we are. Why don't we get rid of that resentment, freeing our minds of it? Releasing our mind and letting God begin to direct our thinking?

Our Steps are to be used not to discuss all these problems but to solve these problems. You and I can get rid of every resentment, if you want to. We can see in the fourth column what we need to change in ourselves, in our personality. Then with God's help, we can change those things.

If I become <u>less selfish,</u> I'm not going to hurt as many people. If I'm <u>more honest</u>, I'm not going to be in hot water all the time. If I get a little more <u>courage</u> instead of <u>fear,</u> maybe I can quit doing some of those things I used to do. And if I can <u>consider</u> other people, then surely my relationship with them is going to be better. If I have <u>less conflict,</u> I'm going to have more peace of mind, serenity, and happiness, and am at less risk of taking a drink.

In Column 4, I have the <u>exact nature of the wrong</u> that I'll be discussing with someone in Step Five. I have those <u>defects of character</u> that I'm going to become willing to <u>get rid of in Step Six</u>. I have those shortcomings that I'm going to <u>ask God to take away in Step Seven</u>.

It doesn't matter if I call them wrongs, mistakes, defects, or shortcomings—they are the things that cause my problems.

REVIEW OF RESENTMENTS

Column 4					
Refer to our List					
Where were we to blame?					
Putting out of our minds the wrongs others have done, we resolutely looked for our own mistakes.	Frightened	Self-Seeking	Dishonest	Inconsiderate	Selfish

FOURTH STEP INVENTORY PROCESS - RESENTMENTS

COLUMN 4 INSTRUCTIONS

THE BEGINNING OF GROWTH: As noted earlier, it is a spiritual axiom that when I am disturbed, no matter what the cause, there is something wrong with me. Now that you have listed and understand the resentment and how it affected you, having stopped blaming or "putting out of your mind the wrongs others had done," you can now look for your own mistakes and learn from them.

Take the following action: Take each person's name or institution from Column 1 of your resentment list and put it in Column 4, and for each one, ask yourself:

1.   What did I ever do to these people on my list at any time in my life (i.e., lie, cheat, steal, manipulate, gossip, use them for my self-centered needs, etc.)?

2.   What wrongs have I ever done to this person at any time in our relationship?

3.   Where was I to blame?

4.   Where have I been at any time in my relationship with this person the following?

FRIGHTENED:
Fear excited by sudden danger. State or habit of fearing; anxious concern about losing something I already have or not getting something that I wanted from this person on my list.

SELFISH:
Caring unduly or supremely for myself, regarding my own comfort in disregard to that of the person on my list.

SELF-SEEKING:
Act or habit of seeking primarily my own interest or happiness without regard to the person on my list.

DISHONEST:
Lacking honesty, willful perversion of truth, or stealing, cheating, or defrauding. Lying by omission, even people-pleasing is living a lie.

INCONSIDERATE:
Not adequately considered; ill-advised, not regarding the rights or feelings of others, thoughtless of the person on my list.

If you are having problems with your Fourth Step, please be sure to call someone in the group or the leaders and share so you won't get stuck or discouraged.

ASSIGMENT: Complete Column 4

WEEK 11 – HOW IT WORKS, PART 5 (Step Four - Fears)

Instructions - How It Works, Part 5

• BIG BOOK Read - Page 67, Paragraph 3 to Page 68, Paragraph 3
• Workbook Read
• Discuss Fears Inventory Process and Fear Prayer
• Review Fear Examples Form
• Review "Review of Fears" Form

ASSIGNMENT: Complete Fears Inventory.

BIG BOOK READ: Page 67, Paragraph 3 to Page 68, Paragraph 3

We're going to start looking at Fears, the second common manifestation of self, the second symptom of spiritual illness, the second thing that blocks us off from God's will. I think we're going to find as we look at fears some of the same things we found with the resentments. First, we're going to see how much fear really does dominate our thinking, and through dominating our thinking, it controls our actions and controls our lives, just like resentments did. I think we're going to find that a lot of our fears stem from something we ourselves have done in the past based upon our old selfish, self-centered, self-seeking character.

If fear dominates our thinking, then God can't. But fear will be just like resentments. We'll not get rid of all fears because fear also serves a useful purpose in life. If we didn't have any fears, we probably couldn't exist at all. We wouldn't be able to walk across a crowded street without getting run over. Fear brings caution and it's useful. But when fear dominates us and causes us to do things that end up bothering other people, or when fear causes us to rationalize our thinking and make excuses for not doing things we should be doing, <u>then fear is really beginning to dominate our life. And, if fear dominates us, God can't.</u>

Fear is the wrong.

That's what separates me from God. But what's the nature of it? I'll find that practically in every case, that if I wasn't so selfish, so dishonest, so self-seeking, so frightened or inconsiderate of other people, if I wasn't so selfish, I wouldn't be putting myself in positions where I have to experience fear. If I wasn't so greedy, I wouldn't be so afraid I'm not going to have enough money. If I wasn't dishonest, I wouldn't steal and write bad checks and tell lies. Then I wouldn't have to worry about what they are going to do with me when they catch me. If I wasn't so frightened in the first place, I wouldn't have to do those things I've been doing. If I was more considerate of other people, I wouldn't be hurting them and experiencing fear.

If I don't change that old character I'm going to have to live with this stuff for the rest of my life—blocking myself off from God's will and eventually go back to drinking. Fears do the same thing to me that resentments do, they block me off from the sunlight of the Spirit.

You can use fear just as you can resentments: To justify not doing things you should really go ahead and do. Most of our fears will disappear when we look at them and see what we have been doing. Those fears that don't disappear, I can also handle with prayer. Then I can change myself and I will have less fear in the future.

FOURTH STEP INVENTORY PROCESS

"ANALYSIS OF FEAR"

FEAR— "Touches about every aspect of our lives."

"Fear" defined: Webster's Dictionary defines "fear" as the feeling of alarm or disquiet caused by the expectation of danger, pain, disaster, or the like. (<u>Being found out, being known for what you know or think you are.</u>) It is said that the driving force in the life of most alcoholics is the <u>self-centered fear</u> that we will lose something we have or that we will not get something we want.

Column 1—Fears.   List all of your fears. We fill this out the same way we did the resentments from top to bottom. I think as we list our fears, we might be amazed at how many fears we really do have.

Column 2—The Cause. Why do I have the Fear?

In Column 2 write a short description of each fear you have experienced. Now, this is not an attempt to psychoanalyze ourselves. Some fears I'm supposed to have. As a child, I was afraid of the dark. As an adult, if it prevents me from going outside at night, then it's an unreasonable fear and I probably need to do something about it. Some people are afraid of heights. But if it keeps me from standing on a balcony of a hotel or on a mountain looking over the side, then it's going to rule and dominate my life entirely and I need to do something about it. I have fears connected with a lot of different things, and most of them have a good root cause, and most of them stem from something I myself have set in motion. When I get them on paper, I can take them to God and ask for help to remove them.

STUDY AND PRAYER:

When our fears have been listed and the above questions answered, the Big Book gives us the solution to fear in the second and third paragraphs appearing on Page 68. We are also given a short prayer. ***"We ask Him to remove our fear and direct our attention to what He would have us be."***

This solution and prayer should be directed toward each of your fears. Check off the box next to each fear, after you have prayed to have it removed.

There is no way to enter into communion with God about fear and at the same time continue to have that fear. We ask Him to remove all our fears and to direct our attention to what He would have us be instead. God will remove that fear—if we ask. I think this is one of the greatest Promises in this Book, it says He will do so; at once, and we commence to outgrow our fears

FEAR EXAMPLES

Fear of:	Why?
Change	Not Changing
Being Alone	Intimacy
Being in a Relationship	Rejection
People	Abandonment
Gossip	The Unknown
Looking Bad or Dumb	Looking Good
People, Male and Female	Sex
Dying	Living
Being Hurt	Hurting Others
Violence	Gangs
Success	Failure
Guns	Diseases
Responsibility	Creditors
Unemployment	Employment
Authority	Confrontation
Theft	Stealing Again
Losing a Spouse, Parent, Child, Friend	Having Children
Hospitals, Needles, Doctors	Police or Jail
Being Found Out	Self-Expression
Street People	Wealthy People
Not Being Liked, Accepted	God
Drowning	Fire
Dogs or Animals	Relapse
Staying Sober	Sin
Someone Seeing Me Cry	Heights
Insects, Bees, Spiders	Government
Physical or Emotional Pain	Religion
Trying Something New	Parents
Getting Old	Insanity
Writing This Inventory	Fear
Faith	Doubt
Money	Poverty

REVIEW OF FEARS

Column 1	Column 2	
The Fears We reviewed our fears thoroughly, even though we had no resentments in connection with them.	**The Cause** We asked ourselves why we had them? Wasn't it because self-reliance failed us?	Page 68 ¶ 3 Prayer

We will be working with the Review of Sex/Relationships form.

Instructions - How It Works, Part 6

• Workbook Read
• BIG BOOK Read - Page 68, Paragraph 4 to Page 69, Paragraph 2
• Workbook Read
• BIG BOOK Read - Page 69, Paragraph 3 to Page 71, End of Chapter
• Workbook Read
• Discuss Analysis of Sex/Relationships Instructions, Columns 1 and 2
• Workbook Read
• Review of Sex/Relationship Form

ASSIGNMENT: Complete Sex/Relationship Inventory; read Pages 72, Paragraph 1 to Page 75, Paragraph 2 (Chapter 6, "Into Action") and start looking for someone to take the Fifth Step with and set a specific date.

Now about sex. Many of us needed an <u>overhaul/change</u> there. We're going to be dealing with how we <u>think about sex/relationships</u> more than how we do sex. This sex thing for humans is quite a bit different than it is with the other animals of the earth. You have to remember that all the <u>other species are God-directed</u>. Whatever they do, whether it be sex, eat or sleep, where they shelter, is <u>all dependent upon God's direction, period.</u>

When it comes time for them to reproduce, God usually signifies that by some change in the female species. There is a physical change. The male of the species senses that change. The male prepares himself and the two join together. Then, they go their separate ways. <u>They really don't have any choice in their sex life</u>. They can't decide when they are going to do it. <u>That's decided by God,</u> usually at certain times of the year, depending on what species they are. They cannot decide who they are going to do it with. They can't decide how many times they are going to do it. They can't decide what position they are going to do it in. For them, it is primarily a reproductive thing, period. <u>It's all done with God's direction</u>.

He made us human beings a little bit different. Because He <u>gave us this thing called self-will,</u> He gave us the <u>ability to think about not only sex</u> but every aspect of our lives also. He gave us the

95

ability to make decisions about it. Of course, He wanted us to use sex for the reproduction of humanity. He also made it very enjoyable for us so we would do it. But then He gave us the ability to choose who we were going to do it with, where we are going to do it, when we were going to do it, how many times we were going to do it, and what position we were going to do it in.

We think that most of the troubles with people sex-wise stem not so much from the physical act itself, as from the way we think about sex. Because through sex we become emotionally involved with every human being. If we couldn't think and reason and have this intelligence, our emotions would not be involved. Most of the trouble that we have is not so much from the physical side of sex, as it is from the emotional or mental side of sex.

What we are going to do by using our Big Book, is to look at our past sex life. We are going to see that some of the things that we have done in the past and maybe still are doing, end up hurting other people. If it does, they are going to retaliate against us, and that in turn is going to cause more pain and suffering for us.

We are also going to find something out, looking at our sex life. That if we're not doing it the way we think we should, or as often as we think we should, it tends to make us irritable, restless, and discontent. And it is very difficult for us to get a handle on a future sex life, where we can be relatively free of worry or fear concerning it. It's like what we had to do with resentments. We had to see what fear really did to us. And now we are going to see what thinking about and having sex really does do to us.

BIG BOOK READ: *Page 68, Paragraph 4 to Page 69, Paragraph 2*

You and I have heard those voices all our lives. They're the ones that say sex is dirty, and you ought to do it one time in one position with one person only, and the only purpose for doing it is to reproduce, and if you enjoy it, there must be something wrong with you. This is the extreme, far to one end of the scale.

I read that last statement in Paragraph 2 with complete relief, because I just knew that this Book was getting ready to condemn me for what I had done in the past and I knew it was getting ready to tell me what I was going to have to do in the future. I had already made up my mind that I wasn't going to pay any attention to it at all, and I was relieved to see that they're not going to do that. And thank God they don't. Because if the Book tried to tell me what was right and what was wrong in the sex area, and what I had to do in my sex life, then the Book could not match human beings anywhere in our world. Our Book is designed to be helpful for any alcoholic anywhere in the world. Thank God it stays out of that kind of controversy.

BIG BOOK READ: *Page 69, Paragraph 3 to Page 71, End of Chapter*

By looking at the past and getting it down and analyzing it, we can develop an idea for the future. Just like our resentments and fears, our sex drive is the same way. It's a great battle, the battle to allow God to help us control these things and find some balance, or these things can dominate us.

We need to <u>always be checking our motives</u> and if they are honest, God will take us to better things. But, if we have <u>trouble in the sex area</u>, Bill gives us instructions to <u>work with others</u>. This will get you out of yourself and quiet the imperious urge and keep you from getting hurt or being hurt.

FOURTH STEP INVENTORY PROCESS

"ANALYSIS OF SEX - RELATIONSHIPS"

COLUMN ONE: "Who did I hurt?"

Let's look at the sheet, <u>REVIEW OF OUR SEX CONDUCT</u>. We make a list of those people we have harmed by our conduct of the past. (**PLEASE NOTE**: The people who harmed you by their sexual conduct should be included in your Resentment Inventory; this Inventory concerns your sexual behavior towards others.) Most of us know exactly what we have done and who we have hurt. There's a thing inside ourselves that usually tells us the difference between right and wrong, between what to do and what not to do. Usually, when we've hurt someone in the sexual area, we know it.

Ask yourself these questions and put a checkmark on the inventory sheet where it applies:

1. Where had I been selfish?

2. Where had I been dishonest?

3. Where had I been inconsiderate?

4. Did I arouse jealousy?

5. Did I arouse suspicion?

6. Did I arouse bitterness?

FOURTH STEP INVENTORY PROCESS - RESENTMENTS

ANALYSIS OF SEX/RELATIONSHIPS – COLUMN 2

COLUMN TWO: "Where was I at fault?"

There are many ways that we can hurt people in the sexual area. Sometimes if we are in a relationship and emotionally involved, as in a marriage, we go outside the marriage. We do things we should not be doing, and our partner finds out about it. We have hurt that individual. We have <u>aroused jealousy, suspicion, and bitterness</u>.

If there are children in the home and our escapades have created problems in the home, then we have harmed our children. If the partner outside the home becomes common knowledge, then they too are hurt. If she is married, we've hurt her husband and her children. With one sexual act, we can hurt four or five or more people very easily.

Sometimes we hurt people simply by demanding more than our fair share. We are using sex to the extent that we must have more and more of it. Maybe our partner doesn't want to do it that much. And we <u>selfishly</u> demand that they do it any time that we want to. And we end up hurting them <u>emotionally, not just</u> <u>physically</u>.

You would think that most of the troubles that we cause for others would come from the <u>sex instinct</u>. Occasionally that is probably true, to get the physical release, the <u>emotional gratification</u> that comes at the moment of successful completion of sex. Maybe we are doing it at the wrong time and in the wrong place with the wrong person. And we <u>hurt each other because of the sexual instinct</u>.

We think that we are going to find in most cases, our <u>sexual harms</u> come <u>not from the sexual instinct</u> but from the <u>social or the security instinct</u>. We found out a long time ago as young boys growing up, that you could use sex to <u>build self-esteem</u>. The more members of the opposite sex you could get the more of a man you were, and some of the girls had the same problem. If that is what we are using sex for, that is not to reproduce humanity, nor to enjoy, it is to <u>build self-esteem</u>, and that <u>falls under the social instinct</u>. Sometimes we use <u>sex to buy emotional security</u>, maybe we are just <u>lonesome</u>. Maybe we just want someone to pay attention to us. We found out a long time ago that we can <u>give sex to buy back a personal relationship</u>, and to build our <u>emotional security</u>. If that is what we are using sex for, that is not to reproduce humanity, nor to enjoy, it is to <u>fulfill the social and security instincts of life</u>.

Sometimes we use <u>sex for material security</u>. Maybe we are in a situation sexually that we would rather not be in. We may find we have become so <u>overly dependent</u> upon that person for <u>material security</u> that we are afraid not to go ahead and do it even though we may not want to do it. If that is what we are using it for, we are using it to <u>build material security</u>, not to reproduce or to enjoy.

Sometimes we use sex to get even with another human being. They go out and do something and that infuriates us, and we say we will show them. Then we go out and do the same thing to get even with them. The fallacy with that is that we can't afford to tell them that we did it. But there we are using sex to get even with another human being, not to reproduce or to enjoy.

Sometimes we use sex to force our will on another human being. They aren't doing what we want them to do, so we say we'll show them. We'll just cut them off from sex. We won't let them have any until they come around to our way of thinking. We boys are not too good at that, we can only last about three days. I will guarantee that you girls have honed it to perfection and know exactly how to use it. Believe me, I would too if it worked that well for me. There we are using sex not to reproduce, nor enjoyment, but to force our will on another human being.

COLUMN TWO (continued): Ask yourself, "What should I have done instead?"

First find out where you were at fault in the situations in your life and then Bill instructs you to ask yourself another question: What should you have done instead? This will help you in shaping a sane and happy sex life in the future by giving you some ideas on what you can do differently next time.

PRAYER, MEDITATION, AND STUDY—Starts on Page 69, Paragraph 2, to Page 70, Paragraph 2

PRAY THIS PRAYER:
We ask God to mold our ideals and help us to live up to them.

INSTRUCTION:
We remember always that our sex powers were God-given and therefore good, neither to be used lightly or selfishly nor to be despised and loathed.

MEDITATION:
We ask God what we should do about each specific matter. The right answer will come, if we want it.

STUDY:
We earnestly pray for the right ideal, for guidance in each questionable situation, for sanity, and for the strength to do the right thing.

ASSIGNMENT: Read Page 72 through Page 75, Paragraph 2. Start looking for someone to take the Fifth Step with and set a specific date.

Review of Sex/Relationships

Sex Whom had we hurt?	Where had we been			Did I arouse?			Where were we at fault? What should we have done instead?	Page 69 ¶ 2 Prayer
	Selfish	Dishonest	Inconsiderate	Jealousy	Suspicion	Bitterness		

WEEK 13 – INTO ACTION, PART 1 (Step Five)

Instructions - Into Action, Part 1

• BIG BOOK Read - Page 72, Paragraph 1 to Page 73, Top of Page
• Workbook Read
• BIG BOOK Read - Page 73, Paragraphs 1 to 3
• Workbook Read
• BIG BOOK Read - Page 73, Paragraph 4 to Page 75, Top of Page
• Workbook Read
• BIG BOOK Read - Page 75, Paragraphs 1 to 3
• Workbook Read

ASSIGNMENT: Complete Step Five with your sponsor. If you are doing this alone, please find a closed mouth understanding friend, doctor, therapist, psychologist, or spiritual advisor and do it at the first opportunity. Also read Step Six and Step Seven in the Twelve Steps and Twelve Traditions book, Pages 63-76.

BIG BOOK READ: *Page 72, Paragraph 1 to Page 73, Top of Page*

is the statement which messed us up in Step Four. We read the phrase "*all* their life story" and then we went back and began to write our life stories. But, as we have seen, 95% of our life story doesn't really have anything to do with our drinking. What does have something to do with our drinking is resentment, fears, and harms done.

If I am listing all my resentments, I am listing all my life story as to resentment. If I list all my fears, I am listing all my life story as far as fear. If I list all my harms done, then I am listing my life story as far as harms done. And it is those things that really count.

BIG BOOK READ: *Page 73, Paragraphs 1 to 3*

Now I'm going to take my inventory to another human being who is not involved in my personal life, who can look at this thing from an outside view and get an objective truthful picture of it. And I let that human being help me see those character defects that I need to get rid of.

I'm amazed at how often my sponsor would change those things on my inventory. He could point out character defects that I was unable to see. He helped me to truthfully look at myself. I know in Step Five, confession is good for the soul. It helps to share these things with someone. The real purpose of Step Five is to learn all I can learn about my self. I need to truthfully see those things that I need to work on and change in the future. Left to my own resources I simply cannot do that.

BIG BOOK READ: Page 73, Paragraph 4 to Page 75, Top of Page

These two paragraphs are as they were originally written in the 1930s. When the Big Book was written, there were no sponsors to go to. Bill was just giving suggestions as to whom to do the Step with. We think it important that one finds <u>a person who has done the work as outlined in this Book</u>. Being knowledgeable as to our inability to be honest with ourselves, they can be objective and help point out our shortcomings.

BIG BOOK READ: Page 75, Paragraphs 1 to 3

My sponsor Ted Harbach says, "<u>this is the most magical page in the book of Alcoholics Anonymous</u>." Page 75 is the beginning of the whole deal. It is sandwiched in between Step Five and Six <u>as a gift from God</u>. There are only two things you can do with a gift. You can take it and make it yours, and <u>be eternally grateful</u>, or you can throw away what I believe to be the greatest gift that God gave to humanity, and it is right there on Page 75.

There are ten Promises on Page 75. It says, "<u>we are building an arch through which we shall walk a free man at last</u>." Freedom for me today is doing what I have to do because I want to do it. There isn't anything in this world I have to do if I don't want to do it, as long as I am willing to pay the price.

It also says on Page 75: "<u>The feeling that the drink problem has disappeared will often come strongly</u>." It says, "<u>Our fears fall from us</u>." You may not know that until sometime later in your sobriety, when you get up the courage to do the one thing that used to terrify you. And then you find out that the fear has been removed from you.

It goes on to say on that page: "<u>We begin to feel the nearness of our Creator</u>" and "<u>We feel we are on the Broad Highway, walking hand in hand with the Spirit of the Universe</u>." My sponsor says, "<u>You will have brushed the face of God and established a conscious contact with a Power greater than yourself</u>." It's all right there on Page 75, and five more Promises. <u>For God's sake, hurry on lest the test comes before you are ready</u>!

ASSIGNMENT: Complete Step Five with your sponsor.

If you are doing this alone, please find a closed mouth understanding friend, doctor, therapist, psychologist, or spiritual advisor and do it at the first opportunity.

While giving your Fifth Step to your sponsor, you will be making a <u>list of your character defects</u> as you and your sponsor have analyzed and discussed them. You may wish to consider purchasing the book, Twelve Steps and Twelve Traditions and then reading Step Six and Step Seven in it, Pages 63 to 76.

Read the first two paragraphs on Page 76 in the Big Book. Look up the definitions of <u>WILLINGNESS and HUMILITY</u> and consider what they mean in context with these Steps.

WEEK 14 – INTO ACTION, PART 2 (Steps Six and Seven)

Instructions - Into Action, Part 2

• BIG BOOK Read - Page76 Paragraph 1 (Step Six)
• Workbook Read
• BIG BOOK Read - Page 76 Paragraph 2 (Step Seven)
• Workbook Read
• Discuss Steps Six and Seven Chart and Suggested Practice of Program Principles

ASSIGNMENT: Read "Into Action" Page 76, Paragraph 3 to page 84 Paragraph 1. Answer homework questions for "Into action" questions. (Steps 8 and 9) Continue to say the Seventh Step Prayer in your morning meditation time.

BIG BOOK READ: Page 76, Paragraph 1(Step 6)

That's all of Step Six. You will notice that he didn't mention "defects of character" in there at all. What he did mention were those things which "we have admitted are objectionable." Now surely in the taking of Steps Four and Five, when we saw resentments, fears, harms done to other people, when we saw that those things stemmed from our basic character defects of selfishness, dishonesty, self-seeking, frightened and inconsiderate character; and when we could see what those things did to us, what caused us to do the things that hurt other people and caused them to retaliate against us and block us off from God, then surely by now those things have become objectionable to us. If they aren't, then the Book, recognizing that self cannot overcome self, says we ask God to help us be willing to have those things removed.

Let's face it, sometimes here at Step Six, even though we see what those old defects of character are doing to us, sometimes we don't want to turn them loose for two or three reasons. Number 1—some of them are fun. Number 2—we don't know what life's going to be like without them. I went to my sponsor and said: "If God removes all my character defects, I won't have any personality left at all." And he said, "You're just about 100% right." But he said, "What you don't understand is that when God takes those away, God replaces them with something better. That something better will be better than you've ever had before, and you are going to have a lot better life by doing so." But I'm still afraid. Sometimes we human beings would rather sit here in today's pain than take a chance of changing for the future because we don't know for sure what that's going to be, and we understand today's pain.

My mind is nothing more than a set of mental habits. Throughout my lifetime those habits have been ingrained in my head. It's automatic for me to react with fear. It's automatic for me to react selfishly and it's automatic for me to react dishonestly. It's automatic for me to be inconsiderate of other people. I don't know how life will be without that. How could I now react differently, because I've never been that way before? Sometimes fear will stop us right here. And if we're not ready and if those things are not objectionable to us by now, then the only thing we can do is ask God to help us be willing to get rid of those things. Slowly, as God takes one away and I practice the other, my character changes. When I take contrary actions against my will, contrary to the way I have always lived my life, I get results that I am looking for sober.

Step Six is a very difficult Step to do. If you want to change, then Step Six says don't do what you want to do, because if you feed action to your old thought patterns and your old character, they're going to grow. But if you don't feed action to your old thought patterns and your old character, they'll die in your mind. And only we can do that. It is not easy, it is very hard.

BIG BOOK READ: Page 76, Paragraph 2 (Step 7)

We have then completed Step Seven. I have found my shortcomings in Step Four. I talked about them to another human being in Step Five and became ready to turn them over to God in Step Six. I asked God to remove them in Step Seven. Now I have completed Steps Six and Seven. Now if I'm not careful, I'll fall into a trap. We tend to feel after Steps Six and Seven that God is going to reach in and pluck out these defects of character and just make us as pure as the driven snow. We turn to God and hand them over and say, "Here you are God, give me the $3.99 special" and everything will be all right. These were not the Steps God took, these are the Steps we took, and we have to change. God doesn't need these Steps, He's okay already.

God cannot reach in my head and remove these character defects without them being replaced with the opposite behavior. If I want God to take away my selfishness, then I'm going to have to start to practice, with God's help and all the willingness I can pray for, to be unselfish. And slowly over a period of time, an old habit can die, and it can be replaced with a new habit. If I'm willing to take away dishonesty, then I'm going to have to try in every given situation with God's help and what little willingness I can pray for, to be honest. Now that's hard for me to do, it's alien to my nature. But, when God helps me remove these character defects and I practice the opposite, slowly the old habit dies, and it's replaced with a new habit.

Sometimes we wind down on Steps Six and Seven because the Big Book only has two paragraphs on these Steps. We begin to see that these are the real tools of change in the Program. Steps One, Two, Three, Four, and Five are seeing the problem and solution and making that decision, and then the inventory, and once we take the inventory, we see these things and then talk them over with another person. The first five Steps give us these two great tools to apply to our lives. Our lives are really based on how we apply these Steps to our lives. God doesn't take these Steps. We must take these Steps. In the twelve Steps and Twelve Traditions on the first page of Step Six, it states, "any person capable of enough willingness and honesty to try repeatedly Step Six on all his faults–*without any reservations whatever*–has indeed come a long way spiritually, and is therefore entitled to be called a man who is sincerely trying to grow in the image and likeness of his own Creator." It says, "Simple, but not easy."

106

DEFINITION OF CHARACTER DEFECTS

The things we do that we know we shouldn't be doing; lying, cheating, stealing, etc.

DEFINITION OF SHORTCOMINGS

The things we are not doing that we know we should be doing: going to meetings, calling our sponsor, paying bills on time, picking up after ourselves, etc.

Review Steps Six and Seven - Practice Program Principles Instead Of Character Defects/ Shortcomings form (next page).

ASSIGNMENT: Read "Into Action", Page 76, Paragraph 3 to Page 84, Paragraph 1. Answer homework questions for "Into Action", six and seven.

Say the Seventh Step Prayer in your morning meditation time.

CHART FOR PRACTICING STEPS SIX AND SEVEN

Character Defects/Shortcomings	Program Principles
Selfish and self-seeking	Interest in others
Dishonest	Honest
Fear	Courage
Pride	Humility – seeking God's will
Inconsiderate	Considerate
Greed	Giving or sharing
Lust	Purity
Anger	Calm – serenity
Envy	Gratefulness
Sloth	Action
Gluttony	Moderation
Impatience	Patience
Intolerance	Tolerance
Resentment	Forgiveness
Hate	Love – empathy
Harmful acts	Good deeds
Self-pity	Self-forgetfulness
Self-justification	Self-acceptance
Self-importance	Modesty
Self-condemnation	Self-forgiveness
Suspicion	Trust
Doubt	Faith
Covetousness	Charity and generosity
Disrespect	Respect

INTO ACTION (STEPS EIGHT AND NINE) QUESTIONS

PAGE 76

1.   Do you have misgivings about these Steps?

2.   Do you feel diffident (distrustful or unduly timid) about going to some of these people?

PAGE 77

3.   What is your real purpose?

4.   Can you approach the people on your Eighth Step list in a helpful and forgiving spirit?

PAGE 78

5.   Do you recognize that nothing worthwhile can be accomplished until you clean your side of the street?

6.   Is it important that you be praised for your Ninth Step efforts?

7.   Do you understand the importance of losing your fear of creditors?

8.   Have you discussed with your sponsor any criminal offenses you may have committed, and which may still be open? If not, you certainly should do so!

PAGE 79

9.   Do you understand how your Ninth Step may harm other people?

10.   Have you studied your domestic troubles and the harm that may have been caused in these areas?

PAGE 81

11.   Do you understand the importance of not creating further harm by creating further jealousy and resentment in a "tell-all" session?

PAGE 83

12.   What does the author mean when he says that the spiritual life is not a theory—we have to live it?

13.   Do you see that in taking the Ninth Step you should be sensible, tactful, considerate, and humble, without being servile or scraping? Are you experiencing the Promises set forth on Pages 83 and 84?

WEEK 15 – INTO ACTION, PART 3 (Steps Eight and Nine)

Instructions - Into Action, Part 3

- BIG BOOK Read - Page 76, Paragraph 3 to Page 78, Paragraph 1
- Workbook Read
- Discuss Instructions for Eighth Step List and for Ninth Step Amends
- Eighth Step Chart for Ninth Step Amends
- Discuss Repairing the Damage - Moving Forward with Forgiveness Form
- BIG BOOK Read - Page 78, Paragraph 2
- Workbook Read
- BIG BOOK Read - Page 78, Paragraph 3 to Page 80 Paragraph 4
- Workbook Read
- BIG BOOK Read - Page 80, Paragraph 5 to Page 83, Paragraph 1
- Workbook Read
- BIG BOOK Read - Page 83, Paragraph 2 to Page 84, Paragraph 1 and review the Twelve Promises after Ninth Step (these are the Promises read in most meetings)
- Workbook Read

ASSIGNMENT: Meet with your sponsor or spiritual advisor and go over your Eighth Step list; read Page 84, Paragraph 2 to End of Chapter; answer homework questions.

BIG BOOK READ: Page 76, Paragraph 3 to Page 78, Paragraph 1

We know that human life emanates from the <u>inside out</u> and there is a <u>design for living</u>. The Big Book talks about this throughout and gives us a design for living that really works. We see that in Step Three, as a result of Steps One and Two, we make a decision, and when we make it for the first time we are in a correct relationship with God in our lives. That's the <u>spiritual foundation</u>. Once we lay that, we go into Steps Four, Five, Six, and Seven where <u>we deal with ourselves</u>. We say that we're a product of our minds, not our bodies. In Steps Four, Five, Six, and Seven we <u>worked on the mind, which is our main problem</u>.

Now we are going out into the <u>third dimension of life</u>, our <u>relationship with others</u>. Now we must go out into that area of our lives and deal with it. We say that alcoholism is an <u>inside job</u>. We started from the <u>inside and we're working out</u>. We're in the last <u>dimension</u>, our relationship with other people. In Steps Eight and Nine, we're going to have to deal with <u>guilt, remorse, shame, and fear</u> which is going to back up into our minds. It's going to <u>cut us off from the sunlight of the Spirit (Steps One, Two, and Three)</u> and we're going to lose all the work we started.

In order for us to <u>complete the job</u>, and completely get rid of those things in our mind that block us from God's will, it's going to become necessary now to do something about that guilt, remorse, shame, and fear associated with the past.

There's no way I can become willing to <u>make amends at all,</u> unless I have really taken a good Step Four through Step Seven, the way our Big Book tells us to do. Even then, some of those people have harmed us as badly as we have harmed them. We can say to ourselves, "They had it coming and I really don't think I owe them any amends." We're going to find a few like that and it's going to be very difficult, even then for us to become willing to make amends to some of those people. <u>If we aren't careful, we'll fall into a trap</u>. We'll say to ourselves, "Since I have not become willing to make amends to them all, then I can't make amends to any of them, period." And <u>Step Eight will block us off entirely</u> from Step Nine if we are not careful.

My sponsor didn't let this happen to me. He said, "Some of these people on your list, you know them and they know you, and you love them and they love you, and you would like to get things straightened out with them right now, wouldn't you?" And I said, "Sure I would." My children were on there, my brother, my mother, my father, and some of my friends. I wasn't sure about Barbara, my wife. He said, "I'll tell you what you ought to do."

INSTRUCTIONS FOR EIGHTH STEP LIST AND FOR NINTH STEP AMENDS

Please open your Twelve Steps and Twelve Traditions to Page 83, Paragraph 2, and it will explain where Joe and Charlie got their instructions for the chart.

When using the chart for the **Eighth Step**, list the people from your Fourth Step inventory, the ones that you are willing to do something about RIGHT NOW, put them in the first column NOW.

Then there are some people in there that you know you're going to make amends to sooner or later. You don't particularly care about it, but you know you're going to do it. Take their names and put them in the second column MAYBE. There are only a few on there that you aren't sure about. You may or may not make amends to them. Take their names and put them in the third column LATER. Now the only ones that are going to be left are those that you don't ever intend to make amends to. Take them and put them in the fourth column NEVER.

Now what I'd like you to do is start making written conversational amends letters to the NOWs. When you have two or three written, call your sponsor, and read them to him or her. In this way you and your sponsor and the God of your understanding can help you make the decisions on how (face-to-face, call on the phone, or send a letter to the person) and when to make these amends.

If the person is dead you might want to go to the grave, if they have one, and make your amends there. Take someone with you so you are not alone when you leave the grave.

Now, by this time you will probably be ready to make some of the MAYBEs.

Once you're through with the MAYBEs, you'll be ready to do some of the LATERs.

Once you're through with the LATERs, you'll be ready to do some of the NEVERs.

My sponsor and my God led me right into this thing and did not allow me to use the fact that I did not intend to make amends to one or two, to keep me from making amends to anybody at all. If you have trouble in this area, you might try this.

It really does work.

EIGHTH STEP CHART FOR NINTH STEP AMENDS

NOW	MAYBE	LATER	NEVER

FORM - REPAIRING THE DAMAGE –
MOVING FORWARD WITH FORGIVENESS

In the first column, write the name of the person you harmed. In the second column, write what you did that harmed them. In the third column, write what you will have to do to make amends.

People that I harmed	What I did that harmed them	What I need to do to make amends

BIG BOOK READ: Page 78, Paragraph 2

After we have become willing, **Step Nine** very clearly tells us what we need to do. It tells us the kinds of amends to make. It says we make DIRECT AMENDS to such people. It tells us when to make the direct amends; except when to do so would injure them or others. The Step itself tells me what to do. The only thing I really need to understand is, what does he mean by "DIRECT AMENDS" what does he mean by "WHEREVER POSSIBLE," and what does he mean by "EXCEPT WHEN TO DO SO WOULD INJURE THEM OR OTHERS?"

Let's start on Step Nine by looking at what he is talking about when he says, "MAKE DIRECT AMENDS." Making direct amends, we're going to look at them in two ways. First, we're going to look at them as direct, face-to-face. That is the best way to make amends. When we make a face-to-face, there's no doubt about what the result is. This thing really does work if we're willing to do what the Big Book tells us to do. It's not easy sometimes to do those things, but the Book continuously reminds us that self cannot overcome self, and we may have to ask God's help to be willing to do these things. I think we'll find the benefits far, far outweigh whatever pain we're going to have in the doing of it.

There are many things that can come up in making amends. That's why we have so much in the Big Book on Step Nine. It has paragraphs that deal with just about everything that could come up. After working with a lot of people, we have never seen anything come up in dealing with making amends, that you couldn't find something in the Big Book to give you some suggestions and actions to take. Now we're going to talk about past criminal offenses, and how we handle those.

BIG BOOK READ: Page 78, Paragraph 3 to Page 80, Paragraph 4

Here again, he considered other people who would be involved, talked to them, got their okay before he made his amends. Undoubtedly, I need to make some amends to my wife or husband. In fact, the only thing I can really do is say: "Look, I know what I was, and you know what I was. I really hurt you while I was drinking and I'm sorry about that, but I'm trying to live a decent life now. With God's help, I don't intend to do those things anymore. And that's about all I can do." And that's about all I can do with my children, too. To most of the people on my list, this is all the amends we can possibly make. Sometimes we feel so guilty we keep beating ourselves up over these things, so we keep on trying to make amends for the same things over and over. Just change the old behavior with the help of God and the Steps. Then get on with your new life.

BIG BOOK READ: Page 80, Paragraph 5 to Page 83, Paragraph 1

There will be some amends that we can never make. Maybe we don't know where these people are; maybe they are dead, or maybe the case would be that it would injure other people. We must live with those. We know we would do it if we could. If we're willing, this will free us. If we're willing, even if we cannot do it at that time, there should be no guilt or remorse or anything to bother us. That's why we're doing all this work.

There's one mistake we see a lot of people make in their zeal to have everybody like them. Sometimes people don't accept our amends. We leave them feeling crushed, and then we tend to want to go back and literally beg those people to forgive us. We don't need to do that. As God's people, we stand on our own two feet. We make our amends to the best of our ability, and if they don't want to accept them, there's nothing we can do about that. All we can do is make our amends.

I think there's one person we owe amends to as much as anybody else, and that's <u>ourselves</u>. I am not about to say that I never hurt anybody with my drinking, because I hurt everybody who came in contact with me when I was drinking. And I'm positive <u>I hurt myself</u> as badly as I ever hurt anybody else. I think the finest amends that I can possibly make to myself is to <u>free myself from the past</u>. The only way I have found to do that is by making my amends to other people wherever I possibly can. Through the making of my amends, my guilt, my remorse, my shame, and my fears associated with the past have disappeared.

BIG BOOK READ: Page 83, Paragraph 2 to Page 84, Paragraph 1

Joe McQ in the Big Book Comes Alive Seminar reads the Promises in the following manner:

This is the way alcohol made him feel before it turned against him:

"When I drank alcohol, I would know a new freedom and a new happiness. When I drank alcohol, I would not regret the past nor wish to shut the door on it. When I drank alcohol, I would comprehend the word serenity and I would know peace. When I drank alcohol no matter how far down the scale I had gone, I would see how my experience could benefit others. When I drank alcohol that feeling of uselessness and self-pity would disappear. When I drank alcohol, I would lose interest in selfish things and gain interest in my fellows. When I drank alcohol self-seeking would slip away. When I drank alcohol my whole attitude and outlook upon life would change. When I drank alcohol fear of people and of economic insecurity would leave me. When I drank alcohol, I intuitively knew how to handle situations that used to baffle me. When I drank alcohol, I suddenly realized that alcohol was doing for me what I could not do for myself.

"My God, no wonder I loved to drink! Alcohol did that for me for many, many years. Alcohol was my friend, I doubt that I could have lived in normal society growing up without alcohol or some other drug, and it did for me exactly what I wanted it to do.

"One day it turned against me. It began to get me drunk, in trouble, and it caused me to do things that I didn't want to do. From that day on I spent the rest of my drinking career searching for a way to drink and recapture the good feelings. Not knowing that I was alcoholic; not knowing that I have a progressive disease; not knowing that there was no way to recapture those good feelings— I almost destroyed my life and everyone else's life.

"I came to AA, and you showed me the <u>Big Book and the first nine Steps</u>. I applied the Steps in my life and to my absolute amazement, I found that I got all the good things from these first nine Steps that I ever got from alcohol. Now if I can feel as good from the first nine Steps as I did from drinking alcohol in the beginning, then I most certainly do not need to take a drink in order to change the way that I feel. I think the amazing thing about it is this: So far, the first nine Steps have never turned against me. I've never been placed in jail because of the first nine Steps. I've never been taken to a divorce court because of the first nine Steps. You see, they have given me all the good things that alcohol gave me, but none of the bad. That's why I don't need to drink. Now if I don't want to receive these Promises, sooner or later my mind is going to start searching for a sense of ease and comfort. It's going to take me right back to the idea that I've got to drink to change the way that I feel. You see, that's what this is about."

Now, why did we get the Promises? We got the Promises because we fit ourselves back into the design for living that God made for us in the first place. When we do that, then we're not in conflict with God, or with our fellow man, or with ourselves, then we can have these Promises. If you'll notice, every Promise in there deals with the mind; none of them deal with the body. Surely if I've had these Promises come true, then I have become a different human being. Surely, if I've received these Promises, my personality has changed entirely from what it used to be to what it is today. We have effectively recovered from a hopeless condition of the mind and of the body at the end of Step Nine, if we have received these Promises.

ASSIGNMENT: Read Page 84, Paragraph 2 to the end of the chapter; Into Action" Steps Ten and Eleven questions.

Try doing your new walk around Step Ten in your daily life and see if you can catch your own character defects and try to correct them as you live your new life One Day at a Time.

Note at this point the Big Book assumes that you made a list of people you had harmed when you did your Fourth Step inventory. If this has not been done, you should certainly make such a list at this point and review it with your sponsor. God will provide the proper time and place if you pray for the willingness to make amends—sometimes quickly and sometimes slowly!

INTO ACTION (STEPS TEN AND ELEVEN) QUESTIONS

PAGE 84

1.   What are the specific instructions outlined for the taking of Step Ten?

2.   What do we watch for?

Note: "By this time sanity will have returned. We will seldom be interested in liquor."

3.   Is this the sanity referred to in Step Two?

PAGE 85

4.   What is the proper use of the will?

5.   What is the suggestion for taking the Eleventh Step on a daily basis?

PAGE 86

6.   What do you watch for?

7.   Do you practice this Step on a daily basis?

8.   Do you follow the procedure outlined on Pages 86 and 87 regarding your daily morning meditations and the way you proceed through the day?

PAGE 87

9.   Has your attitude about a Power greater than yourself changed?

PAGE 88

10.   Do you believe "It works—it really does"?

WEEK 16 – INTO ACTION, PART 4 (Steps Ten and Eleven)

STEP TEN

Instructions - Into Action, Part 4

STEP TEN
• BIG BOOK Read - Page 84, Paragraph 2
• Workbook Read
• BIG BOOK Read - Page 84, Paragraph 3 to Page 85, Top of Page (and review twelve Promises after Tenth Step)
• Workbook Read
• BIG BOOK Read - Page 85, Paragraph 1
• Workbook Read
• BIG BOOK Read -Page 85, Paragraph 2
• Workbook Read

Review Daily Inventory Form for Steps Ten and Eleven

STEP ELEVEN

When We Retire at Night Inventory
• BIG BOOK Read - Page 85, Paragraph 3 to Page 86, Paragraph 1
• Workbook Read, including Nighttime Instructions

On Awakening Inventory
• BIG BOOK Read - Page 86, Paragraph 2 to Page 87, Paragraph 2
• Workbook Read, including In the Morning Instructions

As We Go Through the Day
• BIG BOOK Read - Page 87, Paragraph 3 to Page 88, End of Chapter
• Workbook Read, including Throughout the Day Instructions

ASSIGNMENT: Read Chapter 7, "Working with Others. "We have a daily reprieve contingent on the maintenance of our spiritual condition. If we can continue to do Step Ten throughout our day at work, home, play and catch ourselves and make amends as necessary, and also the Step Eleven, night inventory, morning inventory, and throughout the day inventory, I feel and believe we can stay emotionally and spiritually sober. I believe and have experienced spiritual progress more when I do this practice every day.

BIG BOOK READ: Page 84, Paragraph 2

I think as we leave the first nine Steps, we are halfway through this stage of our development. Then we are about to enter another plane of <u>continuous growth through the last three Steps</u>. A lot of times the last three Steps are called "<u>Maintenance Steps</u>." I think because the word "maintenance" is mentioned over here that we have tied that term on to them. It gives us the idea that we stay where we are. But we like to look at these last three Steps as continuous growth Steps, Steps that we can grow with for the rest of our lives.

We can't really maintain anything as is, everything in the world is changing. The world is under a changing process, whether it appears to be or not. It's either deteriorating or getting better. Like a tree, it's continuously growing and when it stops growing it starts dying. Our lives are the same way. We must continue to grow, and this is what these last three Steps are all about—they are about continuing to grow.

Bill twice in the Big Book mentioned another dimension of living. He talked about the normal three dimensions: the dimension of the spirit, the dimension of the mind, and then our physical, sociological relationship with the world and everything in it. We could see where the first nine Steps had put us back together in the normal three dimensions of living. For just a moment, let's look back on Page 8 in the Big Book and see a reference here of another dimension of living.

Bill says, "I was soon to be catapulted into what I like to call the fourth dimension of existence."

In other words, a dimension of living far beyond the normal three. On Page 25 where he talks about the spiritual experience, again he talks about a <u>fourth dimension of living</u>.

> **"The great fact is just this, and nothing less: That we have had deep and effective spiritual experiences which have revolutionized our whole attitude toward life, toward our fellows and toward God's universe. The central fact of our lives today is the absolute certainty that our Creator has entered our hearts and lives in a way that is indeed miraculous."**

Now just before that paragraph, he says: **"We have found much of heaven, and we have been rocketed into a fourth dimension of existence of which we had not even dreamed."**

There is another dimension far beyond the normal three, that is the fourth dimension of existence. Most people in this world will never even realize there is another dimension of existence. Because they do not have the tools necessary to get them into that dimension of existence. I think we can see that the last three Steps will be growth Steps that will put us into that fourth dimension, far beyond the Promises. There is another spiritual law that applies throughout the entire universe that tells us nothing can ever stay the same. We're going to have to continue to grow, or we're going to begin to regress back.

We can see looking at the Big Book, our textbook, that Step Ten is a <u>continuous practice</u> of Steps Four, Five, Six, Seven, Eight, and Nine. These are the Steps that give us our <u>personality change</u> <u>(growth)</u>. We didn't get any change from Steps One, Two, or even Three. All the <u>change</u> came through the <u>action Steps Four through Nine</u>. The more we take Step Four and see our <u>character</u> <u>defects</u> and then discuss them with other people, the more we'll <u>learn about ourselves</u>. And as we ask <u>God to remove these things</u>, they will become less of a problem for us. As we <u>make amends</u> <u>to other people</u>, our relationships with other people will grow and get better. In the practicing of these Steps, we will not remain the same, and we will grow into the <u>fourth dimension of existence</u>. Step Four has prepared us for this Step. If we don't do a good Step Four, and if we don't learn about our character defects in Step Four, we really can't do a good Step Ten.

BIG BOOK READ: Page 84, Paragraph 3 to Page 85, Top of Page

Everyone talks about the Promises on Pages 83-84, and very few people talk about the Promises here on Pages 84-85. There are <u>twelve Promises after the Ninth Step</u> and <u>twelve Promises after the Tenth Step</u>. These are the Promises we are really looking for when we come to the program.

"AND WE HAVE CEASED FIGHTING ANYTHING OR ANYONE—EVEN ALCOHOL. FOR BY THIS TIME SANITY WILL HAVE RETURNED."

Remember we said in Step Two—<u>Came to believe that a Power greater than ourselves</u> could restore us to sanity. Remember that insanity didn't mean we were crazy. We were <u>insane in one area</u> when it comes to <u>alcohol</u>. Let's see how we are looking at <u>alcohol</u>, now. Remember that little piece that was missing? It's going to come home to us now. Back on Page 45, it said the "<u>main objective is to enable you to find a Power greater than yourself which WILL solve your problem</u>." We emphasized then, that it doesn't say—which will <u>help</u> us solve it or will <u>enable</u> us to solve it.

It says, **"<u>WHICH WILL SOLVE YOUR PROBLEM.</u>"** Somewhere between Page 45 and Page 85, I woke up one morning and I said, "There's something strange in my life today, I don't want to drink." And I said, "How long has it been since I've wanted to take a drink?" And I couldn't remember. Somewhere between Pages 45 and 85, God reached in my head and He plucked out the <u>OBSESSION TO DRINK ALCOHOL</u> and it's never returned. God replaced the <u>OBSESSION TO DRINK</u> with the <u>OBSESSION TO STAY SOBER</u>. This obsession is a good one. It will allow me to see the truth and that truth will be so strong, that it will overcome the idea to drink. God did that for me and I believe this is the real <u>miracle of Alcoholics Anonymous</u>.

BIG BOOK READ: Page 85, Paragraph 1

In that paragraph, you will see the word "maintenance" and it is done only <u>ONE DAY AT A TIME</u>. The rest of this paragraph shows us the proper use of the will. It doesn't say anything about saying to God: God, where shall I work? Or, God, tell me who I ought to be married to. Or, God, show me a sign. This says, ***"How can I best serve Thee—Thy will (not mine) be done."*** When this obsession to drink is removed entirely and if we received these Promises, for the first time in our life we are in a position where we can really serve God and our fellow man. And, unless we are willing to do so, chances are we're going to end up losing what we have anyway.

I love the idea of exercising our willpower along this line all we wish. We made a decision in Step Three to turn our will and our lives over to the care of God as we understood Him. In Steps Four through Nine, we removed enough self-will that our minds became pretty well normal or straightened up. Now that we can use our will properly, they have given us our will back here at the end of Step Ten. But I'd like you to notice the perfect sequence of the Big Book. They give us our will back on Page 85, but they restored our sanity on Page 84. We'd have been in bad shape if we had received our will back before we got our sanity back.

BIG BOOK READ: Page 85, Paragraph 2

We are talking here in this paragraph about a sixth sense of direction. Most of what we know, we learn through our normal five senses of direction. For instance, everything I know today on a conscious level, I learned through hearing, seeing, tasting, feeling, or touching. That's the only way we human beings have of learning anything. We gather information from our five senses and that information lodges in our mind at a conscious level. Then we use that information to run our lives, and we almost destroy ourselves.

If God dwells within all human beings, and I'm convinced He does, and God has all knowledge and all power, then that means that you and I have within ourselves all the knowledge and all the power that we could ever possibly need to solve any problem.

Because through the Steps we learn to tap into that Power and let that Power solve our problems.

Human beings have known forever that the way to do that is through prayer and meditation. Most of us alcoholics have problems with prayer and meditation. Even though I was raised in the church, I found when I came to AA, I knew very little about prayer and nothing at all about meditation. I had two prayers, one was "Now I lay me down to sleep" and the other was "God, get me out of this damn mess and I swear I'll never do it again." The only other prayer I knew was "God, if you'll do this, I'll do that." I always tried to bargain with God. Today I realize God's got the controls and doesn't need to bargain with me at all.

Let's see if we can find a way to tap into that unsuspected inner resource of strength and see if we can't continue our spiritual growth through Step Eleven.

Daily Inventory

Step 10 & 11

When we retire at night, we constructively review our day.
Were we Resentful, Selfish, Dishonest, or Afraid?

Personality Characteristics of Self-Will

- ☐ Self & Self-Seeking
- ☐ Dishonest
- ☐ Frightened
- ☐ Inconsideration
- ☐ Pride
- ☐ Greed
- ☐ Lust
- ☐ Anger
- ☐ Envy
- ☐ Sloth
- ☐ Gluttony
- ☐ Impatience
- ☐ Resentment
- ☐ Hate
- ☐ Harmful Acts
- ☐ Self-Pity
- ☐ Self-Justification
- ☐ Self-Importance
- ☐ Self-Condemnation
- ☐ Suspicion / Jealous
- ☐ Doubt

Personality Characteristics of God's Will

- ☐ Interest in Others
- ☐ Honesty
- ☐ Courage
- ☐ Consideration
- ☐ Humility-Seeking God's Will
- ☐ Giving or Sharing
- ☐ What we can do for Others
- ☐ Calmness
- ☐ Gratitude
- ☐ Take Action
- ☐ Moderation
- ☐ Patience
- ☐ Tolerance
- ☐ Forgiveness
- ☐ Love, Concern for Others
- ☐ Good Deeds
- ☐ Self-Forgetfulness
- ☐ Modesty
- ☐ Trust
- ☐ Faith
- ☐ Sponsorship

STEP ELEVEN

BIG BOOK READ: Page 85, Paragraph 3 to Page 86, Paragraph 1

If we have taken Steps Four through Nine and continued to take the same actions in Step Ten on a daily basis, we should have removed the things that block us off from God and our fellow man. Now we should be able to receive God's will, to tap that unsuspected inner resource of the Spirit. That's what all the Steps are about—to get us to Step Eleven. Once we work Step Eleven, then we can carry this solution to another person. Step Eleven is the pinnacle (summit or the highest point according to Webster's dictionary).

When I got to this section of the Big Book, I was amazed by what Bill wrote, because he was not a spiritual giant at this point. Bill was only three years sober, he had been around the people of the Oxford Group and his wife Lois would read to him from the Bible. Now here he was, faced with the task of writing something on prayer and meditation. He didn't have that ability and he was writing to a group of people that were spiritually bankrupt. I am glad and thank God he did not have a great spiritual life. Most people who are founded in theology and in spiritual education talk over the heads of people who are spiritually bankrupt.

He lays out a <u>simple daily plan</u> that anybody can <u>adopt and apply</u> to their lives. Anybody who will take this plan in Step Eleven and apply it to their lives, will teach themselves a personal life of prayer and meditation. In the first paragraph, Bill is going to tell us what to do <u>at night</u>. Anyone who can see this outline, apply it on a daily basis, regardless of whether you are spiritually bankrupt, will tap into the unsuspected inner resources of the Spirit. You will be able to <u>see God's direction</u> and develop this <u>sixth sense of direction</u> in a personal way on a daily basis. We see now that this thing we do at night is in Step Eleven, not Step Ten.

STEP ELEVEN AT NIGHT INSTRUCTIONS

This is the only place in the Big Book that it tells you a specific time of the day to do something. When you ***retire at night*** it gives you specific instructions. It says to constructively review your day as follows:

1. Ask yourself if you were resentful, selfish, dishonest, or afraid? **Step Four**
2. Was I kind and loving toward all?
3. Was I thinking of myself most of the time?
4. Was I thinking about what I could pack into the stream of life?
5. Was I thinking about what I could do for others?

It tells you what <u>not to do</u>: Don't worry and have remorse, don't get into morbid reflection, because you won't be any use to others.

6. It asks if you have kept something to yourself that needs to be discussed with another person and, if so, to talk to someone at once? **Step Five**
7. Ask yourself if you owe an apology? **Steps Eight and Nine**

Then after you've done the review it gives you a Prayer:

I can ask God's forgiveness and inquire what corrective measures should be taken.

It is almost impossible to do this and stay the way you are. Most of the <u>successful people</u> I've ever met tell me that one of the reasons for their success is this <u>ability to stop and inventory themselves</u> <u>from time to time</u>. I find it takes less time and energy to do this <u>every evening</u> than it does to wait until I get real, real sick. Sometimes these things sneak up on me slowly and I get into two or three little problems and don't do anything about them, and tomorrow I pick up another one or two, and the next day three or four. Then a week or so later I am <u>sick</u>, and in bad shape, and it <u>takes a lot</u> <u>of work to dig out of that mess</u>. This daily inventory keeps me realizing the things I need to do in order to continue to grow.

BIG BOOK READ: Page 86, Paragraph 2 to Page 87, Paragraph 2

We humans, how do we do in the morning? We get up in the morning, begin our day, and we have to go take a shower, then comb our hair, then women have to put their faces on, and men have to shave. Then we get down to that important stuff, what we're going to wear, shoes, belt, underwear, etc., and this takes a lot of time. Maybe we eat, and then we run out and check our car and we go off to work for the day.

I wonder what we have done about <u>our lives and our minds</u>. I often wonder what our lives would be like if we humans would spend as much time on our minds as we do on our clothes. <u>Our minds</u> <u>run the whole show</u>. It takes time, it takes that <u>quiet time in the morning</u> to get our lives together. It says, "<u>Our thought-life will be placed on a much higher plane</u>." We have great minds, I've never seen a dumb alcoholic. I ask myself, is my life as good as my mind? NO! I have a better mind than my life, because it seems like there's something always blocking me from the real quality of life. When I stop in the morning and have that quiet time, I find that my thinking gets better. When my thought-life gets better, then my thinking is cleared of wrong motives and my life improves.

STEP ELEVEN IN THE MORNING INSTRUCTIONS

Each morning, we think about the twenty-four hours ahead.

1. We think about our plans for the day. Suggestion: Make a To-Do list.
2. We ask God to direct our thinking.
3. We ask that our thinking be divorced from self-pity, dishonesty or self-seeking motives.
4. I think about my day and if I have any indecision, it tells me to ask God for inspiration, an intuitive thought, or a decision.
5. Now it says to leave it up to God, to let go and relax and take it easy, and don't struggle.
6. It says that if I do this, I will be surprised how the right answers are going to come if I continue to do this for a while.

It tells me that <u>I just meditated,</u> and I didn't even know that was what I was doing. It gives me another prayer to pray.

It goes like this: I ask to be shown through the day what my next step is to be, that I will be given whatever I need to take care of my problems. It tells me to ask especially for freedom from self-will, and to be careful to make no request for myself only. It tells me to ask to be helpful to others and to be careful to never pray for my own selfish **ends.** ("Ends" in the dictionary means the <u>result</u> of something, like a red car, new house, etc.) In just a short period of time, if I would take this incredibly good and definitely valuable suggestion, it will completely change my life. The thing that makes this really effective is to use all these suggestions together each day—not just a morning meditation or just a night meditation, we need to do both.

Paragraph 1 on Page 87 deals with prayer. Here we are going to begin to work on an effective prayer life. Remember, Step Eleven says we pray "<u>only for knowledge of His will for us and the power to carry that out</u>." It takes time for us to develop effectively praying just like that. That's what we need in our lives as alcoholics who have lost their way in life, through our undisciplined lives. What we really need is God's direction in our lives and the Power to carry that out. It's very difficult to fashion that type of healthy prayer life; it takes time and work.

Now we are going to talk about our personal lives, and a personal communication with God, God as we understand Him, to deal with our specific lives and our specific problems. We must fashion a prayer to fit God as we understand Him and say our needs as we see them to God. And surely as alcoholics, we have lost direction. The only thing we need to pray for is <u>God's direction in our lives</u> and the <u>power to carry that out</u>. Anyone who will use the valuable suggestions that Bill has laid out for us here should be able to develop a specific prayer life to focus on our specific needs, and our specific problems on an individual basis. We will see that God's direction in our life will grow and God's will, will become very clear.

BIG BOOK READ: Page 87, Paragraph 3 to Page 88, End of Chapter

STEP ELEVEN THROUGHOUT THE DAY INSTRUCTIONS

Throughout each day we have to face indecision. The instructions in the Big Book are as follows: We pause (stop, pray, time-out) when we get agitated or doubtful, and we ask God for the right thought or action. "<u>Thy will be done</u>."

We have to begin to realize that we are human. That's the biggest thing wrong with us is that we happen to be human. And we're on the face of this earth for only a short period of time. During the time that we are on the face of this earth, we experience some things and we learn some things. We don't know it all and we're going to face things each day that we don't know what to do about. I think one of the greatest gifts this program has given me is the ability to say, "<u>I don't know, I just don't know</u>." And that is a very hard thing for a self-centered person to say.

God has a covenant with me, He will allow me to struggle based on self-knowledge or I can let go and plug into His Ultimate Source of information. And it is found within every one of us. When I relax and take it easy and I say I don't know, then I am free to operate on other things that day. When I have a problem I cannot seem to do anything about, I can now listen to other people and know that God uses other people to speak to me, and they may have the answers.

Our Book says, "What used to be the hunch." We all have hunches, but they come when they want to, seemingly. But by practicing this definite and valuable suggestion, the occasional inspiration gradually becomes a working part of the mind. If we practice this, it will be something we can always use to receive answers in our lives.

This one will change your life. But you need to practice and practice.

ASSIGNMENT: Read Chapter 7, "Working with Others."

We have a daily reprieve contingent on the maintenance of our spiritual condition. If we can continue to do Step Ten throughout our day at work, home, play, and catch ourselves and make amends as necessary, and also do the Step Eleven-night inventory, morning inventory, and throughout the day inventory, I feel and believe we can stay emotionally and spiritually sober. I believe and have experienced spiritual progress more when I do this practice every day.

Read Chapter 7, "Working with Others." This whole chapter is devoted to Twelve Step work because "faith without works is dead." Start thinking about what you will be doing to be of service to God and your fellow man in a Twelve Step manner. We hope you will pair up with someone in the Workshop and pass it on.

WEEK 17 – WORKING WITH OTHERS (Step Twelve)

Instructions - Working with Others

• BIG BOOK Read - Page 89, Paragraphs 1 and 2 (First Part of Step Twelve)
• Workbook Read
• BIG BOOK Read - Page 89, Paragraph 3 to Page 98, Paragraph 2 (Second Part of Step Twelve)
• Workbook Read
• BIG BOOK Read - Page 98, Paragraph 3 to Page 103, End of Chapter (Third Part of Step Twelve)
• Workbook Read
• BIG BOOK Read - Page 164, A Vision for You
• Workbook Read

BIG BOOK READ: Page 89, Paragraphs 1 and 2

Let's look at Step Twelve for just a moment. There are three parts to it: **The first part**, probably the greatest Promise to be found anywhere in the Big Book – "Having had a spiritual awakening as the result of these steps." I think that is a promise to me, if I will put the first eleven Steps to work in my life to the best of my ability, that then I can have a spiritual awakening.

What is a spiritual awakening? It is a personality change sufficient to recover from alcoholism. Bill tells us in the Twelve Steps and Twelve Traditions there are as many kinds of spiritual awakenings as there are people in AA. But they all have certain things in common. That is, they are able to feel, believe, and do things that they could never do before on their own strength unaided. If that is the criteria for a spiritual awakening, then I believe I must have had one of some kind, because I certainly feel things that I never felt before.

Today I feel true love. I never knew what love was. I always had love mixed up with sex and things like that. Today I realize that doesn't have anything to do with love. Love is compassion, tolerance, patience, and goodwill towards my fellow man. Today I feel some of that. Before AA, I never felt any of that and I could have cared less about you. You could have some after I got what I wanted, but I was going to get mine first every time. Those feelings have changed.

Today I believe things I never believed before. I believe God is a kind and loving God. I believe He stands ready to help any human being anywhere in the world, the instant they are ready to give self-will back to Him and begin to follow His will. Before, I thought God was Hellfire and Brimstone. I believe God disciplines us; sometimes we are so hard-headed that it takes a big blow to us to get our attention. I think we are the ones that punish ourselves, not God, and we blame how we feel on Him. My belief about God has changed entirely. I can do things that I couldn't do before I came to AA; I can stay sober. I could never do that before; and because I'm sober, I'm allowed to do many, many things I could never do while I was drinking. If that's the criteria, then surely, I've had some form of spiritual awakening.

BIG BOOK READ: Page 89, Paragraph 3 to Page 98, Paragraph 2

Now the second part, what am I supposed to do with it? Carry this message—not <u>a</u> message, not <u>the</u> message, not <u>some</u> message, but <u>this</u> message to others. What is this message? Having had a spiritual awakening as the result of taking these steps. That's the only message that we have to carry to other people. Sometimes we get to thinking we're healers in AA. Or we get to thinking we're marital advisors, economic advisors, sex advisors. I don't know of any group of people in the world that screwed that mess up worse than we did, yet we think we can advise other people in those areas. NO WAY!

"<u>But the ex-problem drinker who has found this solution, who is properly armed with facts about himself, can generally win the entire confidence of another alcoholic in a few hours</u>." We know more about it than anybody alive because we're the only people in the world who have experienced the disease of alcoholism. Same thing with the recovery process, we are the only people in the world who have experienced recovery from the disease of alcoholism.

Now we can take that unique knowledge and carry that to another human being and help them understand what their problem is—<u>the disease of alcoholism</u>. Help them understand what their solution will need to be—<u>a vital spiritual experience</u>. Help them walk through a <u>Program of Action</u> with the help of this Workshop and the people that started it. They also can have a <u>spiritual awakening and recover</u> from their disease. And we are the only people in the world who can do this.

I've got to believe that in the 1930's, God got tired of seeing people like us die. He had to take Bill and Bob and Ebby and Dr. Jung and Dr. Silkworth and the Oxford Group, and all the others concerned, and put this thing together. God has always worked with people through people. Very seldom does He speak to one of us directly.

If God worked through people in the 1930's to set this up, and now they're all dead, it stands to reason that He'll work with people today and, through people, continue to carry this message to those who are still suffering. There's no alcoholic in this room that shouldn't be dead. How many times did we wake up the next morning and say, weren't we lucky the night before?

I don't think luck had anything to do with it. I think we're a chosen people. Not as a race, but to do a job. They tell me today that 96-97% of the alcoholics that are alive today will die from their disease, never even knowing that they're alcoholics. Three or four percent of us manage to stagger into AA and less than 25% of us are recovering. Now we're talking about one out of one hundred who have recovered from this disease.

I used to say, "God, why am I an alcoholic?" Today I say, "God why am I not one of those dying from the disease?" I don't have any trouble with God's will. I don't think God is concerned with where I work. I don't think He's concerned with where I live. I doubt whether He's concerned with who I am married to, to any great extent. I think there is one thing He is concerned with: what am I doing with what was given me so freely? If we can take this unique knowledge and together avert death in countless thousands of people, I think we will be very lucky individuals.

BIG BOOK READ: *Page 98, Paragraph 3 to Page 103, End of Chapter*

The third part, in Step Twelve, says, "We practice these principles in all our affairs." Well, what are the principles? We've heard arguments go on for hours about this, just like the difference between a defect and a shortcoming and a wrong. In How It Works, Bill said:

> **"No one among us has been able to maintain anything like perfect adherence to these principles. We are not saints. ... The principles we have set down are guides to progress."**

What did he set down just before that statement? The Twelve Steps of Alcoholics Anonymous. In the Forward of the Twelve Steps and Twelve Traditions, he says,

> **"A.A.'s Twelve Steps are a group of principles, spiritual in their nature, which, if practiced as a way of life, can expel the obsession to drink and enable the sufferer to become happily and usefully whole."**

I have never seen him yet write about the principles, except when it was in connection with the Twelve Steps. They are a set of principles. Now it's easy for me to practice them here in AA. I love you and you love me and we're going to do our best not to hurt each other. And through practicing these principles here in AA – that one hour a day—we can be happy, peaceful, and free. But what do we do with the other 23 hours a day?

I practice these principles in my own home 10-12 hours a day. And I practice these principles with my spouse. I realize how powerless I am over her. I realize the insanity of this. She's 53 years old. She's not going to listen to me anymore. I decide to turn her will and her life over to the care of God as I understand Him. And I inventory myself to see why I still have the need to control her. I find those defects of character that cause that, and I talk it over with another human being and I ask God to take them away. And I make amends quickly to her when I have harmed her. There are times I'm ashamed of myself. There are times I treat absolute strangers with more courtesy than I treat my own spouse in my own home. If I practice these principles in my home with her, I could be happy, peaceful, and serene for another 8-10 hours a day.

How about with my children? Can I realize how powerless I am over them? Can I realize the insanity of me trying to control their lives for them? My oldest child is 33, the youngest is 28. They're not going to listen to Daddy anymore. Can I decide to turn their will and their lives over to the care of God, as I understand Him? Can I inventory myself and see why I need to control them? Can I find those defects and do something about it? Can I make amends quickly when I smart off to them once in a while? If I could practice these principles with my children, I could be happy when I'm with them. If I don't do this, I don't stand a chance with them, because all we'll do is argue and fight. If I can practice these principles with my kids, I can be happy another hour or two a day.

How about on the job? Can I see how powerless I am over my coworkers? Do I realize the insanity of me trying to control them? Can I make that decision, and take inventory of my behaviors on the job? If I have wronged someone, can I make amends? If so, then I can be happy another 8 or 9 hours a day. We're down to about 23 hours now.

I have one hour left. How about the supermarket check-out line? I'm in the express lane, I've got 3 items. There's a little old lady in front of me with her whole basket full. She has about 50 things in there. She shouldn't be in this damn line anyway, she needs to be over there. I'm in a hurry and I want to get through here. Now it takes them about 10 or 15 minutes to add up her bill. Then after they add up the bill, she pulls out her coupons. It takes another 10 minutes to add up her new bill, and they get her new bill added up and she gets out her checkbook. It takes her about 10 minutes to write the check, and then she stands there and balances her checkbook. She shouldn't be in this line in the first place and I'm in a hurry. Now, if I could practice these principles in the supermarket check-out line, I could be happy there, too.

What we are saying is, it's really up to us how happy we are. We have the tools, haven't we? We've got eleven Steps and if we will use them in our lives on a daily basis, we can be happy, peaceful, and serene 24 hours a day, 7 days a week, 4 weeks out of the month, and 12 months out of the year. If we choose to do so. But it's entirely up to us. Nobody else can do it for us, and nobody should do it for us. We'll have to do this with God's help, for the rest of our lives if we want to be happy, peaceful, and free.

BIG BOOK READ: Page 164 - A VISION FOR YOU. *It is a fitting way to end your Step work.*

This is how Joe and Charlie read it:

Our book is meant to be suggestive only. We realize we know only a little. God will constantly disclose more to you and to us. Ask Him in your morning meditation what you can do each day for the man who is still sick. The answers will come if your own house is in order. But obviously, you cannot transmit something you haven't got. See to it that your relationship with Him is right, and great events will come to pass for you and countless others. This is the Great Fact for us.

Abandon yourself to God as you understand God. (We did this in Steps One, Two, and Three.) Admit your faults to Him and to your fellows. (We did that in Steps Four, Five, Six, and Seven.)

Clear away the wreckage of your past. (We did that in Steps Eight and Nine.) Give freely of what you find and join us. (We do that in Steps Ten, Eleven, and Twelve.)

We shall be with you in the Fellowship of the Spirit, and you will surely meet some of us as you trudge the Road of Happy Destiny.

May God bless you and keep you—until then.

SUGGESTION:

Find some new members of Alcoholics Anonymous and share this Workbook with them.

Chapter 8, "To the Wives," Chapter 9, "The Family Afterwards," Chapter 10, "To Employers," and Chapter 11, "A Vision for You," are all chapters to teach you how to practice these principles in all your affairs. These chapters contain many spiritual truths which apply to all of us and should be read.

PASS IT ON!

Charts for Reproduction

The following charts are included for you to remove and make copies as needed.

YOUR GRUDGE LIST

PEOPLE	INSTITUTIONS	PRINCIPLES

REVIEW OF RESENTMENTS

Column 1	Column 2	Column 3									Page
I am resentful at	The cause	Which part of self is affected									67
		Social			Security			Sex			¶ 1
		Self-Esteem	Relationship	Ambition	Material	Emotional	Ambition	Acceptable	Hidden	Ambition	Prayer
We listed people, institutions, or principles with which we were angry.	We asked ourselves why we were angry.										

REVIEW OF RESENTMENTS

Column 4					
Refer to our List					
Where were we to blame?					
Putting out of our minds the wrongs others have done, we resolutely looked for our own mistakes.	Frightened	Self-Seeking	Dishonest	Inconsiderate	Selfish

REVIEW OF FEARS

Column 1	Column 2	
The Fears We reviewed our fears thoroughly, even though we had no resentments in connection with them.	**The Cause** We asked ourselves why we had them? Wasn't it because self-reliance failed us?	Page 68 ¶ 3 Prayer

Review of Sex

Sex Whom had we hurt?	Where had we been			Did I arouse?			Where were we at fault? What should we have done instead?	Page 69 ¶ 2 Prayer
	Selfish	Dishonest	Inconsiderate	Jealousy	Suspicion	Bitterness		

EIGHTH STEP LIST FOR NINTH STEP AMENDS

NOW	MAYBE	LATER	NEVER

Repairing The Damage – Moving Forward With Forgiveness

Step Eight list of persons harmed, what I did and what to do to make amends

In the first column, write the name of the person you harmed. In the 2nd column, what you did that harmed them. In the 3rd column, write what you will have to do to make amends.

People that I harmed	What I did that harmed them	What I need to do to make amends

Made in the USA
Las Vegas, NV
29 April 2024